A SONG FOR GRANDMOTHER

Ministering to the Elderly

by

Dorothy Miller

© 1990 by Jeremiah Books

Published by Jeremiah Books

Hemet, California, 92343

Printed in the United States of America

Scripture quotations are taken from the King James Version of the Bible.

Library of Congress

Cataloging-in-Publication Data

A Song For Grandmother

Miller, Dorothy

TABLE OF CONTENTS

ACKNOWLEDGMENTS

Thanks be to God for allowing me to share the blessings and call of ministering to the elderly. He used many people to bring this book into existence. Thank you, Lord, for my mom's example, for Dawn's prompting, for Wendy's patient deciphering, for Milo's suggestions, and for Biola's Writers' Institute information. Also, Lord, you were so good to have brought Barbara, Lela, Ruth, Colleen and Don in to fine tune, Pat and Caryl in to believe, and my family to support.

FOREWORD

Say not ye, there are yet four months, and then cometh harvest? Behold, I say unto you, lift up your eyes, and look on the fields; for they are white already to harvest (John 4:35).

People, old and feeble, are isolated and largely forgotten by the Christian community. It's because of these forgotten ones that this book is written. They need our visits. These pages offer information to prepare for this adventure and encouraging stories that highlight the blessings.

After reading this book, you may feel overwhelmed by the needs of the elderly. Remember, RESPOND ONLY TO GOD'S PERSONAL CALL TO YOU, NOT TO THE PERSUASION OF OTHERS.

How Jesus must have agonized as He walked on this earth some 2,000 years ago. He saw need in every direction. People thronged him for help, but He could not minister to all of them. Did He fail? No. Jesus prayed in the garden, *"I have finished the work which thou gavest me to do."*

God always deploys his workers in the best possible way. If visiting is not your calling, please pray for the elderly and the people who are called to minister to them. However, if God impresses you to go to the elderly, GO! Expect to bless and to be blessed.

Perhaps, one day, we will meet in some hallway as we serve.

SECTION I

The Need

Elderly citizens residing in professional care homes have many needs. Even if these seniors receive nutritional meals and live in attractive, clean surroundings, their needs are not necessarily met. They, like all of us, have social, emotional and spiritual needs that must be addressed.

This section unveils unmet needs and suggests who can help. It also tells about different types of professional care homes and some of the reasons for their existence.

Chapter 1

IS THERE A NEED?

Ruth, an eighty-seven-year-old woman, bedridden and blind, greeted me warmly as I entered her room for the first time. "Do come in," she said. "Come, sit on my bed and visit."

As I launched into singing "Love Lifted Me" accompanied by my supportive autoharp, she joined in softly. Upon finishing, she scolded me for leaving out the third verse.

"That's the best one," she said. "Don't leave it out." Since I didn't even know that verse, she sang while I strummed along. What a delight! It was quite apparent that Ruth loved the Lord and had walked many years with Him.

We chatted awhile, speaking of Jesus and how He had sustained us both throughout our lives. Then abruptly, she took on a more serious expression and questioned, "Why is it that after eight years of living in rest homes, the pastor of our church has only visited me once, and he only did that after I requested him to? Doesn't he know what Jesus said? *'I was a stranger, and ye took me in; naked and ye clothed me; I was sick and ye visited me.'"* [2]

Ruth apologized, "I'm sorry, I can't remember exactly where that is in the Bible, but I do remember that Jesus said that *'inasmuch as ye have done it unto one of the least of these my brethren, ye have done it unto me!'"* Turning to me with her sightless eyes, she pleaded, "Doesn't my pastor know what the Bible says?"

Sadly, I couldn't give her an answer. Her question has continued to haunt me. Perhaps her pastor is so occupied overseeing a large church that he cannot spend time ministering to such individuals. If that is the situation, then shouldn't some of his church members assist him by spending time in visitation? No matter who is at fault, the somber fact is not one person from Ruth's local congregation takes time to visit her.

I continued pondering Ruth's question and the words of Jesus that she had quoted. Perhaps the members of Ruth's local church are not the only people who neglected her. Isn't it true that all believers are born into the same family (the body of Christ) to which Ruth belongs? The Lord made clear to me that day that we, the Christians, have ignored the needs of people in these "dying places".

New babies are wrinkled and red, have wet diapers and very little hair, yet we adore them and say how cute they are. Why then, after a life of service to others, do we regard the elderly as wrinkled, useless and a burden?

Is our reluctance toward involvement with the aged due to our value system? Do we worship youth, vitality, strength, position and wealth? Are we afraid to see people whose bodies are in decline because we want to pretend these gathering places of the old simply do not exist?

In the Bible, God presents His will concerning these needy oldsters.

> *"Comfort the feebleminded, support the weak, be patient toward all men."* [3]

Certainly many aged and needy people benefit from the services provided by homes for the elderly. However, the use of these homes changes the family structure by removing the aged and dying from our homes and visible presence. This large group of displaced people who have only a short time left on earth have become separated from the vital contact of family and friends.

As the body of Christ, we need to obey the Lord. Some of us must follow the elderly to these homes, where most residents will spend their final days. By visiting these forgotten ones, we can offer the love and support that God has directed us to give.

Chapter 2

WHO IS QUALIFIED TO GO?

The director of Social Services in a four-hundred-bed facility told me, "The average patient spends three years in long-term care. We try to fill the patients' lives with interesting in-house activities, but they also need contact with the outside world. Of course the carolers come at Christmas and sometimes Scout groups will come as a community service project. There are also church groups that arrange to come in and run services once a week. The residents really love this." She added, "Would you believe, though, that sometimes the residents are all lined up in their wheelchairs ready for the services and the church people don't show up?"

"When they do come," I asked, "are they able to spend time with individuals after the service?"

"No, not usually," she answered. "Mostly they come on Sunday afternoons after church and I think they need to hurry to get back to evening services."

"What about volunteers who come in on their own?" I inquired.

She shook her head. "In the ten years I have worked here, there have been only three volunteers who visit regularly.

"Dorothy, at every regional meeting, we discuss the problem of the lack of volunteers in long-term care facilities. We have no answers." Scrutinizing me with a frustrated expression, she asked, "Do you have any ideas?"

"Yes," I thought to myself, "I do have an answer. As Christians, we must respond to the need."

There are many reasons why we have not responded to these needs. Some Christians feel that only special people can participate in this ministry. They assume only outgoing, multi-talented individuals with years of experience in witnessing, could minister to the elderly.

These hesitant Christians have a deep desire to serve God in some way, but their feelings of inadequacy inhibit them from trying any type of service. They don't realize that ministering to the elderly can help to diminish these feelings of inadequacy. Actually, nursing homes are one of the easiest places to begin personal evangelism.

Other people avoid visiting because they "can't stand to see those people, it's so depressing!" Unfortunately, one of the unconscious prejudices many people harbor is ageism. It produces the feeling that elderly people are less valuable than younger ones.

These negative feelings change when you go representing the Lord. You begin to see each person as an important individual, just as God looks at us.

God reached out to us because of His love. I am forever grateful that He cares for us even though He saw that we were "unattractive" sinners. God's Word says, *"Christ died for the ungodly."* [4] We, in the Christian community, must strive to reach out to the residents of nursing care homes in the same loving manner.

Still other Christians are simply unaware of any need to befriend the elderly. They are under the impression (since no one at church mentions visiting) that the elderly population has no need.

Is it possible we have all been assuming that someone else is caring for these shut-away seniors?

A percentage of Christians knows the need and also realizes God could make them adequate for this service; however, they genuinely are not called to go there. These obedient believers are actively serving the Lord elsewhere.

One more type of Christian comprises the group to which I used to belong. My hesitation to visit was for still another reason. I will never forget how it all started some seventeen years ago...

"Paul, let's make a cute little house out of these old Christmas cards."

Three-year-old Paul climbed into my lap and together we selected just the right cards for our project. This particular craft brought joy to my Pioneer Girl group so now I wanted to construct one with my firstborn child.

We threaded the yarn in and out and connected the sides. Next, we laced the bottom card onto the sides and last, we fastened the roof.

"This is the part we leave open, Paul, so that we can put things inside." I led his small fingers in finishing the weaving so he would feel that he had made the house.

"Mommy, what are we going to put in this box-house?"

"I don't know yet, Paul. Why don't we try to think of something."

Several days went by before the right idea came to me. It was nearing Christmas. I could use the empty box-house to teach Paul the value of giving. My husband and I had always agreed that we didn't want our son to grow up thinking the real meaning of Christmas was how many presents he got. We both grew up in loving but lean circumstances, so we recognized the temptation to shower our son with the gifts we had dreamed about as kids.

"Paul, I've thought of what we can put in our box-house! Let's bake some yummy cookies and put them inside. Then, we can give the box-house to some nice, older person who doesn't have any friends." I smiled as Paul became interested in the project. "You know Paul, there are some people who don't live in the same kind of house we do; they don't even have a family. Wouldn't it be fun to give someone our box-house for a Christmas present?"

He agreed, and so we prepared for our **one-time** visit to experience the "real" meaning of Christmas.

This project served another purpose. Besides teaching Paul, it would please my mother. For several years, my mom and my mother-in-law had been visiting a friendless woman in a local nursing home. They had invited me along but I had politely declined. Although I hadn't told them why I wouldn't go, the reason seemed obvious. I believed that if you didn't have much ability and were too old to help in really meaningful Christian service, it was fitting to visit old, senile people in rest homes. Certainly, I reasoned, if the Lord had given me leadership abilities, He wouldn't want me to waste them on people who couldn't do anything. Besides, I was a riding instructor, an outdoor person not the "type" to deal with people in beds and wheelchairs.

God was patient with my immature evaluation. In time, He showed me a completely different picture of who I was and a whole new concept of the people inside professional care homes.

To arrange our visit, I telephoned the same nursing home my mom visited. I asked if any older people lived there who never had any company. They recommended a patient named Millie. She had no surviving family or friends and they thought she would probably love company.

We arrived on visiting day with our box-house full of cookies. Frankly, I wasn't that confident, but Paul seemed eager and after all this trip was mainly for him anyway.

We entered Millie's room, which she shared with three other ladies. The roommates seemed to be sleeping so they didn't even notice us as we entered. The nurse made introductions and left us standing by Millie's bed. Millie appeared to be about eighty years old. She was bedridden and at least a hundred pounds overweight.

"Hello, Millie. My name is Dorothy and this is my son, Paul."

I nudged Paul and he handed her the box-house of cookies. She smiled at him and took the cookies.

I thought to myself, "This is going very well." Then I inquired, "How are you?"

She replied, "How are you?"

I said, "Fine, thank you."

She said, "Fine, thank you."

I said, "It's raining a lot today."

She said, "It's raining a lot today."

After several more attempts at conversation, it became apparent that Millie could only repeat whatever she heard.

I silently prayed, "Help, Lord! How can we visit with an echo?" In desperation I decided to try to say something about God. I just couldn't think of anything else to do. After a few shaky words, I started to quote John 3:16. What a shock! She interrupted and quoted the entire verse to us, faster than I've ever heard scripture spoken. Afterwards, she sat there, propped up against her pillows, smiling happily. After further experimentation, I found that she knew lots of scriptures and could quote each one in the same rapid fashion.

What an unusual person she was. Paul and I had never met anyone like her before. That day we both fell in love with this smiling, Bible-quoting old lady.

Each week, we returned to visit our new friend. She began to recognize us and occasionally was able to carry on a real conversation.

During the early days of visiting, no one was there to give any "dos and don'ts" or ideas on how to visit successfully. I made lots of mistakes but, thanks to God, none of them were life-threatening.

As time went on, Paul and I spoke to the other ladies in the room. They seemed to enjoy the attention and we always enjoyed talking to them. Soon we were peeking into other rooms and asking, "Would you like some company today?"

I met residents who were thrilled to have some "company," because they had outlived their own friends and relatives. A few patients were fortunate enough to have someone who lived close enough to visit regularly. Others sat in wheelchairs looking out the window, waiting for relatives who never came.

I was unsure at first in this new environment so my conversations only occasionally included mention of the Lord. In time, however, this changed. It became easier and easier to comfortably and naturally speak of Jesus.

The Lord even showed me how an inner longing of mine would be fulfilled as I learned to minister to these seniors. I'd always wanted to sing, but whenever I stood before an audience, my throat constricted and breathing became a prime concern. As I strained to finish each line of the song, I would promise myself never again to sing in front of people. The pressure was too great.

This all changed when I tried singing to the elderly. I soon realized there was no "pressure". The seniors loved and appreciated visitors, so the constricting concern about personal acceptance lifted and freedom to live as God designed took over.

What a innovative Lord we have! He produced growth and involvement in a whole new ministry using just a box-house made of cards.

Everyone is qualified to go. We all have something to offer whether it's friendship or talents. Being qualified to care for our neighbors is not a gift of the Spirit reserved for a chosen few. If God calls you to visit, the ability to serve is already yours.

The Bible says,

> *"Let every one of us please his neighbor for his good to edification."* [5]

Also we are told in James that personal involvement with those in physical need is a demonstration of the reality of our faith. [6]

Chapter 3

WHERE ARE THESE PLACES AND WHY DO THEY EXIST?

A comment made to me by an intelligent sparkling lady residing in a nursing home, holds great significance. She said, "You may find this hard to believe but until my family brought me here I never even knew these places existed." Sadly, most people are not aware of the more than two million Americans residing in long-term care facilities.[7]

There are many factors unique to this century that have swelled the population in elderly-care homes. In previous centuries, the elderly citizens who had no one to take care of them, were relegated to the dreaded "poor house". Now, due to benefits from medicare, medical, and health insurance programs, the ailing and displaced seniors have financing to pay for their care.

These funds, of course, have encouraged construction of facilities for the elderly. In 1960, total revenue in the United States from the nursing home industry was $500 million. By 1974, the intake had risen to $7.5 billion. Then only 14 years later in 1988, this revenue had ballooned to $20 billion, 258 million![8]

There are other factors causing a higher percentage of our citizens to spend their last days in professional care homes. These are a result of changes that have taken place in our society.

It's not uncommon for elderly family members to have disorders, either mental or physical, that make living alone too dangerous for them. In this situation, it is desirable for offspring of the aging parent to arrange things so their parent can live with "family". However, if all the grown children work during the day, providing care for aging parents can present a real problem. Unfortunately, it is often not financially feasible for anyone to stay at home with an aging parent.

Others of these two income families either are not willing to accept the inconvenience of caring for a failing parent or they have no interest in giving up the affluent lifestyle that two incomes provide.

With no one at home to watch grandmother or grandfather, institutional living for the elderly becomes an often-used resource.

The number of families in the U.S.A. where both husband and wife work outside of the home has soared in this century. In the year 1890, 4.5 percent of the married women were working outside the home. By 1978, this percentage had risen to almost 50 percent.[9]

Another change yet that relates most directly to ministering to seniors, is our society's attitude toward old people. Historically, younger people have drawn on the older ones in their family clan for wisdom and knowledge. Now, because of our high-tech methods of problem solving, we simply do not have the same respect for the wisdom of our elders. Many people believe that older citizens who can't participate in our accelerated space age, should simply get out of the way. Admittedly, these thoughts have always existed to some degree, but never to the extent they exist today. This setting-aside, particularly of older men, can be graphically demonstrated. In the year 1890, 74 percent of the men over sixty-five were still in the work force. There has been a drastic change in this number which had dropped to 17.5 percent by the year 1988.[10]

FIRSTHAND INSIGHTS

Tremendous insights as to how we feel about our elderly population surfaced when Pat Moore revealed her experience in the book, "Disguised".[11] She devised a plan to supplement her studies in gerontology and industrial design. Her plan was to transform herself into an old lady by applying theatrical makeup, binding her body into a bent position, and donning appropriate oldster's clothes . She felt, in this way, she could experience the life of an older person firsthand.

During her masquerade as an elderly lady, she felt the fear and helplessness common to seniors who live in big cities. Her experiment even brought her to the place where she nearly lost her life during a mugging. The insights she gained and shared in her book demonstrate the average person's disregard for senior citizens.

Several of Pat's observations are particularly important to those who intend to minister to the elderly. The

instant transformation, from being a vivacious twenty-
six-year-old to becoming a senior citizen, was a shock.
The patronizing, uncaring, and sometimes cruel treatment by people who believed her to be elderly, made
her bristle and want to strike back verbally.

At first, it was very hard for Pat to understand why
the authentic seniors she met did not speak up for their
rights and fight back. After awhile, she began to realize the reason for their lack of resistance. Genuine
senior citizens arrive in the "elderly bracket" over a
period of years. During the slow aging process, unfair
and patronizing treatment comes on a little at a time.
These people, continually treated as incapable and
having no value, gradually come to accept the evaluation as truth.

When you deal with elderly citizens relegated to institutional living, you begin to recognize how these
oldsters are living out society's opinion of them. Because the seniors learned gradually that no one any
longer values their feelings and ideas, they simply
cease to venture forth mentally and physically. They
withdraw into depression and early senility, and give in
to mistreatment and neglect.

I saw people treat my own kind, wise father in a
patronizing manner during his last years. After observing this demeaning attitude firsthand, I began to recognize the extent of the prejudice felt toward older
people.

The real eye-opener came for me, however, when I
discovered myself feeling the same way about an
oldster I met in a nursing home.

That afternoon, I sat beside a gentleman who told me
an episode from his life. He was charming. As he

spoke, I saw in him a resemblance of my own deceased father. Something in my brain registered, "This is somebody's father!" Before that moment, I had been spending time with him because he was a poor, lonely old man. Now, somehow he was different. He was a gentleman, someone much older than I, to whom my respect was due. It wasn't that I had ever been rude to any of the people I visited but rather that I'd harbored an inward attitude of condescension. I discovered that I saw myself as being extremely thoughtful to listen to their antiquated stories.

As I experience the privilege of spending time with these older people, the Lord continually reshapes and reveals my pockets of prejudice.

PROFESSIONAL HOMES ARE VITAL TO SOME FAMILIES

There are some critics who suggest that families who move relatives into a professional home are not acting responsibly. In actuality, some families simply cannot provide the kind of care their aging relative requires. The decision may be based on economics, space limitations or an inability to provide adequate supervision. Sometimes conflicting personalities or even the wishes of the patient indicate that living apart from the family is the best decision. Most families use the services of professional care homes only when absolutely needed.

WHAT AND WHERE ARE THESE FACILITIES?

As God directs you to minister to the elderly, it is surprising to discover the abundance of facilities near your home. In nearly every community in the United States, there are establishments which house the elderly and infirm. Check the yellow pages under Rest Homes. You'll see numerous listings such as Board and Care, Retirement, Intermediate Care, Nursing Homes, Rest Homes, Convalescent and Skilled Nursing. The major types of facilities are Nursing, Retirement, and Convalescent.

NURSING HOMES

Nursing Homes may offer long-term care, both skilled and extended. These classifications have to do with how much medical attention is provided for the patients. The residents include several groups.

Some of the patients are seniors who formerly lived in retirement residences. Most retirement homes require occupants to be able to walk to a central dining area. If because of physical breakdowns, residents need medical care or can no longer commute to meals, they must move out of the retirement home. Their needs, however, are not serious enough to necessitate admittance to an acute-care hospital. Other residents are those who because of mental debilitation cannot care for themselves.

RETIREMENT FACILITIES

The tenants of Retirement Residences, or "Board and Cares", are usually mobile. These are older people who have chosen to gather in a community setting where housekeeping, cooking and maintenance are, at last, someone else's responsibility.

Some of these tenants still enjoy excellent health but are financially unable to live on their own. Many people desire to live in this environment. Others have no one willing or able to provide a home for them.

CONVALESCENT HOSPITALS

Convalescent Hospitals offer several types of care. Patients just released from acute-care hospitals go into the skilled care section of the building. Some of these patients improve and return to independent living. Rehabilitative services such as physical, speech, and occupational therapy assist in recovery.

Other sections of the building may house patients in various stages of mental or physical decline who need light medical supervision. These hospitals often offer board and care living quarters.

IN CONCLUSION

1. As you begin your ministry of volunteering, it is helpful to recognize the different kinds of facilities.

2. Seek to understand the emotions and needs of the elderly residents of these homes.

3. Continue to monitor your own evaluations of the seniors to whom you will minister.

Chapter 4

WHAT GOES ON INSIDE?

STAFF YOU WILL MEET

Most long-term care facilities demonstrate concern for their residents. The majority of the staff works hard, showing true dedication. Occasionally, however, you'll discover, a home whose employees begrudge working with the elderly and infirm. Here the lack of love and attention is readily apparent. Immediately on entering a poorly-run facility, you notice the residents will not return a smile. Many of these oldsters just sit or lie in zombie-like states. Frequently in these places, even the smells accost your senses.

Some of these establishments employ a high percentage of non-English-speaking aides. This tends to heighten the patients' feelings of isolation. Envision yourself separated from your family. Now imagine your feelings each day, as the people who attend to

your needs never speak to you. If your other roommates are senile or too ill to converse, you are in a type
of "solitary confinement". Soon you will retreat into
your own inner world and be classified as senile.
Once, upon entering such a place, I was amazed by the
head nurse's reaction to me when I requested permission to visit and sing to the residents.

"Why would you want to do that?" she muttered.
Before I could formulate a reply, she shrugged her
shoulders and walked away, saying, "Go ahead, I don't
care."

This home harbored a noticeable atmosphere of
despair. Nevertheless, God's name was honored that
very day. One sweet eighty-two-year-old lady, after
hearing the Gospel for the first time, prayed and asked
Jesus to be her Savior. Praise God! He's still on
the throne even when circumstances look their
bleakest.

In well-run homes, you will receive encouragement
from the management and most of the staff. They care
deeply for the residents.

Most people employed in professional care homes
are quite aware of emotional needs of the residents'.
Unfortunately, as the staff works their shifts, they don't
have much time to stop and listen to stories or hold a
lonely grandmother's hand.

The activities director of a senior citizens' home told
me how she felt about volunteers coming in to visit.

"Volunteers are pure gold as far as I'm concerned."

"But what about volunteers who only come in occasionally?" I asked. "Doesn't it disappoint people if
we don't come regularly?"

"Oh sure, it's really nice," she replied, "if you can come at the same time every week. That way they can look forward to your visit. But you know, when someone just drops in and sings or chats with my people, it's great. After the volunteer leaves you should see the smiles on the resident's faces. They feel loved and they realize they're not forgotten."

"How do you feel...," I wondered aloud, "about my speaking to them of God?"

"Oh," she replied, "the residents love it. You realize, of course, that this is not a religious home so I can't say much, but most of the residents are really interested in those types of discussions. A volunteer is much more able to talk about those things than any of the staff."

Keep in mind as you make your way down the hall and into the rooms that you could be perceived as a troublesome outsider by some staff members. To insure your continued welcome in a professional care home, don't disturb the staff. Especially in the beginning, it's normal to notice situations you think should be changed. Your first reaction is to summon a nurse or aide to quickly right the wrong. Be cautious. Wait before you rush in to correct a perceived wrong. Realize that calling a professional over to do something that you feel is important is implied criticism. This often has a negative effect on their performance.

In most instances, you'll have the best chance of affecting change in a thoughtless worker by your ministry's demonstration of God's love. Also, the very presence of outsiders has a positive effect on the personnel not functioning up to a decent standard.

Most staff members do adequate to excellent work. You will, of course, notice that some workers exhibit more tenderness and consideration than others. Unfortunately, this is true of people whether they work with the elderly or not. Observe as you visit. Gradually, you will learn about caring for the elderly.

After you become an experienced, accepted volunteer, you may notice a situation that you know needs immediate attention from a staff member. Then your suggestions will be appropriate.

PHYSICAL DESIGN OF HOMES

As you enter a home, it's helpful to know the basic design of most facilities. The floor plans of **nursing** and **convalescent** homes include a pleasantly-decorated foyer and a dining room that doubles as a meeting room. The hallways have nurses' stations, occasional alcoves and resident rooms on both sides. Most rooms house two or three people. A night stand and a closet are provided for each resident.

Many **retirement** residences exhibit lovely decor. These showplaces advertise auditoriums with high quality sound systems. The management offers games, leisure sports and planned activities on a regular basis. Each tenant resides in a room quite like a small apartment.

If the size of most professional homes seems intimidating, look for a facility in your area which houses only five to fifteen people. Perhaps the smaller size and family atmosphere will appeal to you as a place to serve.

IF THERE IS NO HOME NEARBY

Some communities may not be large enough to support a long-term care facility. If this is the situation in your hometown, there are still ways you can minister to elderly and shut-in citizens who live in their own homes.

Seniors who cannot drive are deeply appreciative of your phone calls and visits. They are grateful for assistance with shopping, or any other gesture that demonstrates concern for them as a friend. Remember God says his people are to be responsible for the needs of the stranger, the fatherless and the widows. [12]

Even if you are unable to travel or find any shut-ins close by, there are still avenues of service open to you. By telephone or letter, contact the nearest professional care home. Tell the social director of your desire to befriend residents who do not have visitors. Administrators know the value of outside contact and thrill at your interest in their residents. The letters and greeting cards you send these lonely people will be read, re-read and displayed on their walls for months.

MORE HELP TO COME

Does all this sound exciting? It is, and these few suggestions are really just a beginning. In this book I'll relate encounters of amazing nursing home visits. Also included are scripture helps and practical ideas. As you read on, you'll discover even more steps you can take toward having your own rewarding Christian ministry among some of God's most beloved children - the senior citizens in your community.

Chapter 5

WHY ME?

PURPOSES YOU CAN FULFILL

So much can be accomplished by your visits. Many of the homes' residents have known the Lord for more years than you've been alive. They love to talk about Him. They also have an acute awareness that they are about to embark on the most exciting trip of their lives. They need to share this excitement with a comprehending friend.

As you seek to befriend these special people and bring joy into their lives, you will receive many rewards. You'll discover some new friends who, as saints of God, will greatly bless you. These precious ones have walked with the Lord so long that God's words in Proverbs- *"But the path of the just is as the shining light, that shineth more and more unto the perfect day"*- have become a living reality in them.[13]

Unfortunately, there are others who know the Lord but have not walked close to Him, nor are they familiar with scriptures about heaven and life hereafter. They need you to encourage them and to give them comfort through God's Word.

ENCOURAGING WORDS

Sometimes while visiting you'll meet residents who voice frustration. They feel shut away from any possible useful purpose. They candidly suggest, "Why can't I just die now? My life doesn't mean anything to anybody. I'm old and I want to die." One helpful response to residents in this frame of mind, is to encourage them to consider the needs of their "neighbors".

I had occasion to reassure one despondent believer by asking her if a missionary's chosen life could be described in this way: moving away from home to a foreign place, obeying God by telling others of His love, praying for the needs of the local people and helping tangibly when they were able. She agreed. Then I asked if she could consider herself a "missionary" to this nursing home.

She mused a moment and then brightened as she responded, "Why yes, I suppose I could."

"See, you have an important opportunity here," I said. "Remember, in the Bible, God suggests that in whatever circumstance we find ourselves, we are to be content.[14]   God needs all of us who understand his message to share it freely with the people we contact. Living in a nursing home is not your choice but you could look for avenues of service to others on this 'foreign' soil.

"God says you can still expect to be productive and 'bring forth fruit in old age.'[15] He also tells us to 'redeem the time'".[16] Smiling at the bedridden lady I asked, "Do you see in that verse that we are never to retire from using our time wisely?"

She smiled. "Well I suppose If you look at it that way, I could speak about God to the nurses or my roommates. I could pray more too, 'cause one thing I got in here is TIME".

STILL TIME FOR COMMITMENT

Sadly, some residents have never made a personal commitment of faith in Jesus Christ as Savior. They just haven't given God much thought. Others have depended on their religion or "churchgoing" to make them acceptable to God.

Continually remind yourself that as long as there is life in an individual, there is still time to receive salvation by faith. Years of self-guidance and denial of God's plan of salvation bring a certain hardness characterized by despair and fatalism.

Remember, though, in the Bible we read that everyone on earth has an awareness of God. [17] Through the help of the Holy Spirit, you can stir this awareness. Perhaps you will enjoy the privilege of introducing some people to their Savior, Jesus Christ.

OTHERS ARE INFLUENCED

Another exciting facet of conversing with the residents about Jesus and God's Word is that on-duty staff and visitors may overhear you. They may be hearing biblical truths for the first time!

You will also discover staff members and nurses that are already Christians. They do appreciate the support and fellowship of visitors who are Christians.

EXAMINE OUR OWN VALUES

When we spend time with people who, because of age, no longer seek material possessions, promotion, prestige or status, we find our own values tested. If we base our lifestyle solely on this world's standards, we have only shallow words of help to offer the elderly. How strange that, even as Christians, we sometimes deny old age and death. It simply interferes with the permanent-feeling lifestyle we have set up on earth.

God knew we would have a tendency to do this, so Jesus warned us by using the following contrasts. He said not to accumulate earthly treasures which can grow old and rusty or be stolen. He told us rather to lay up treasures in heaven as they can't be stolen or corrupted there. He went on to explain, *"Where your treasure is, there will your heart be also."* [18] We see this emphasized again in another verse. *"Set your affection on things above, not on things on the earth."* [19]

The truth is that most Christians feel awkward even being around the elderly. This is because the values by which so many Christians live, offer no real hope. If this is your situation, please don't despair. There is hope for you just as there is hope for them.

The Bible depicts aged believers as potentially wise and useful. *The Bible Speaks on Aging* by Frank Stagg is a well-done compilation of the scriptural view of aging. If you are struggling with your own aging process, Frank Stagg's book will help you.

In the Resources section of this book, you will find a list of other useful books dealing with the practical, emotional and spiritual problems of aging.

IMPORTANCE OF FACING
THE REALITY OF DEATH

The need to become comfortable with God's viewpoint of life and death has two purposes. First of all, you will be encouraged to become a volunteer. Secondly, the elderly face death on a regular basis, and they need your support.

This second need was demonstrated to me during one visit. A darling wheelchair patient confided in me that day, "I've been here two years, but I don't have many friends.

"I can't understand that, Ethel," I replied. "You have a great personality."

Anxious to help her, I assumed she was just shy and needed help in meeting some of the other residents. "Here," I coaxed, "let me introduce you to a wonderful Christian lady I just met."

Ethel dropped her head and whispered, "Oh, I don't think so. It's too hard to make friends. They go in and out so much."

After a bit of coaxing, she did eventually decide to meet the new lady. They managed to get along quite well together.

As I left that day, a sobering question began to haunt me. Was Ethel referring to the difficulty of cultivating new friends, only to have them move away or was she saying, in veiled language, "It's too painful to make new friends only to lose them through death"? The reality of the situation struck me. These homes are dying places. Not only are people living with the knowledge that this may be their last earthly home, they are also experiencing additional pain each time a friend dies. Ethel was avoiding adding possible grief by simply keeping to herself.

Again, the Lord impressed me with the value of volunteers. Friends from the outside become particularly valuable because the risk of losing them through death is not as high. The value of visiting the elderly is underlined by the fact that there is only one time in the Bible that God speaks positively of religion. It's found in James where He says, *"Pure religion and undefiled before God and the Father is this, To visit the fatherless and widows in their affliction."*[20]

SECTION II

How To Visit

This section will help you discover your gifts and how to apply them to a ministry of volunteering. It also provides specific information to help you become a successful visitor. Stories of actual visits are included to give you a firsthand picture of what you may encounter.

Chapter 6

USING YOUR GIFTS

Have you ever read the list of gifts in Romans 12:6-8? It's exciting to realize that God in His perfect workmanship has designed everyone with a special ability. Study this list because your gift can produce everlasting benefits if used in His service.

- Prophecy (forthtelling, speaking God's message with boldness),

- Ministry (rolling up your sleeves and performing tasks for others),

- Teaching (having a natural love and ability to convey ideas),

- Exhorting (gifted at saying the right words to encourage others),

- Giving (loving to share money and goods with others),

- Ruling (being a natural administrator or organizer),
- Mercy (enjoys personal involvement in helping people).

One might assume that only a person with the gift of mercy could minister to the elderly. Not so. Each one of these gifts listed in Romans can support the needs of the elderly.

Let's see how your gift might operate in some of the following situations.

Some elderly residents are physically well enough to venture from their retirement or nursing home, but they need transportation. You could drive them to the store or treat them to lunch. These short trips mean so much to shut-ins! Try offering to drive them to church meetings. Belonging to an outside church body, bolsters their self-image as well providing Christian fellowship.

MINISTERING TO THOSE WHO CANNOT TRAVEL

For those physically restricted to their professional care home, you may either:

- bring in programs,
- be an impromptu visitor, or
- involve others.

1. IDEAS FOR PROGRAMS, WEEKLY AND OC-CASIONAL

a. Church Services.

Establishments welcome the outside groups who provide programs for their residents. Since many of the residents have been regular churchgoers all their lives, they appreciate these "in house" church services. Begin by leading a lively song service (many homes have a piano or organ in their meeting room). Then follow the format of a regular church service. You might have prayer, announcements of interest, and a message from the Bible. You may feel prompted to be the speaker. If not, then invite members of your own church to teach on a rotating basis. Be bold. If necessary, contact Christians from other congregations to present the Word of God. Sunday afternoons are an ideal time to provide these "church" meetings. "Nursing Home Ministry"[21] is an excellent resource. It contains detailed Christian programs designed for the elderly.

b. Bible Studies.

Many residents, whose bodies are failing, have excellent minds and still love to learn more from God's Word. Most Christian bookstores offer a wealth of good Bible study materials. Use your Sunday School quarterly. Teach the residents favorite truths you have recently learned. These study times, different from structured church programs encourage discussion within the group.

c. Story Telling.

The concentration and mental capabilities of some oldsters may be somewhat limited. If you encounter this situation, just tell a Bible story using visual aids. Flannelgraph figures or overhead projectors are fun and effective methods to present God's truths. When residents appear limited in their ability to comprehend, communicate on a basic level. Love them. Never patronize. Keep stories simple, clear and not too long. Use lots of body movement and be animated and excited as you speak. They'll love it!

d. Song Services - What Fun!

Have an old fashioned hymn sing. You'll probably discover, as they gather around and sing with you, they know more of the good old hymns of the church than you do. Sing along with tape recorded music. Use the home's organ or piano as accompaniment. Find a helper who plays a portable instrument such as a guitar, autoharp or accordion. These instruments help, but are not essential if you sing out to get everyone started.

Make lists for yourself and have lots of songs to choose from. Some residents can read, others can't. Use of books, sheet music or lyrics on poster boards may help, but often it takes away from spontaneity. Avoid asking these people to learn many new songs. Oldsters feast on the songs they've known and sung for years. If you do wish to introduce a new song, be sure to choose one that is very easy to learn. Select one with lots of repetition.

e. Christian Crafts.

If working with handcrafts is your specialty, why not organize a weekly time of instruction and fellowship with home residents. Most older people have developed quite a few handwork skills. Whether it is knitting, sewing, tatting, crocheting, needlepoint, painting, leather or clay, all crafts can be done to the honor of the Lord. The Bible says, *"Whatsoever ye do, do heartily, as to the Lord, and not unto men."* [22] Whatsoever means crafts, too.

The projects these people produce may be presented to the needy in the community. These crafts could also become gifts for other residents in the nursing home. Organize crafts that fulfill God's guidelines for living. God tells us to put God's Words literally in front of our eyes so we can see them as we walk, talk, eat and rest. [23] Again in Proverbs, God says of His Words,

> *"Bind them continually upon thine heart, and tie them about thy neck. When thou goest, it shall lead thee; when thou sleepest, it shall keep thee; and when thou awakest, it shall talk with thee."* [24]

Be clever. Invent ways to paint or sew Bible promises to hang on residents' walls. These people spend countless hours lying in bed or sitting in the solitude of their rooms. What an uplift to see a verse and remember God's unchanging love!

Some residents have not yet committed their lives to Jesus, and perhaps don't even know how. The process of permanently inscribing a Bible verse could lead them to a knowledge of God's will.

If you begin a craft with a resident, avoid letting another more capable patient finish it. Crafts, however simple, are one of the few areas in which the elderly can still feel a sense of being worthwhile.

Assist them but don't take their handwork away. These crafts are an extension of the person creating them. Why wound a fragile resident by suggesting, "Someone else could complete this craft better than you"?

f. Non-weekly Programs.

Sometimes due to other commitments, you cannot establish a weekly visit. There are still ways to serve. You or some of your friends may have the ability to sing, act, speak, do puppet shows or tell stories. Arrange ahead of time with the home's staff to have a special performance to share the talents you possess. Use posters and flyers to encourage attendance as well as to provide the necessary program information.

Using young converts from a home Bible study, we formed a group to sing in nursing and retirement homes. We sang accompanied by lively "split track" tapes such as Mother Goose Gospel [25] and Hymns for Kids. [26] These tapes project the instrumental music from one stereo speaker and the recorded voices singing from the other. By turning the volume low on the voice-side the kids learned the songs easier and were more likely to sing on key when they performed. We called ourselves "The Light Company".

As we sang, the residents began to smile and clap to the lively, spiritual songs. We choreographed some of the songs so   the youngsters could sashay in and out among the wheel chairs.

A favorite moment came when three children from the singing group stepped out into the audience and each stood by a resident. We would then ask the audience to join in and sing, He's Got the Whole World in His Hands. On successive verses, I'd call out to one of the youngsters in the audience.

"Stacy, who else does God have in his hand?"

At this point Stacy, had already asked the resident's name. She would call back, "This is Minnie."

We then clapped and sang a verse to Minnie,

He's got Minnie here in His hands,

He's got Minnie here in His hands,

He's got Minnie here in His hands,

He's got the whole world in His hands.

Oh, if you could only see the beaming faces of each chosen celebrity!

Our program included everything from my six-year-old daughter singing "Jesus Loves Me" to a cappella duets by some of the adults. We included a few familiar hymns sung by the audience and performers together.

At the conclusion of our program, we "mingled" with the residents. It is important, as well as rewarding, to speak individually to those in attendance. Then, you not only entertain, you also demonstrate your interest in the residents as individuals. Since we sang only of the Lord, it was natural to continue to speak of Him as we mingled.

Some patients would ask, "Do you really believe what you sing about?" Often the residents would grasp our hands and say, "You've lifted my heart today," or "I was so depressed, but not any more."

After that, we went from room to room visiting those who couldn't, or hadn't, come to our program. While in the rooms, we would chat awhile or hold a wrinkled hand and say to the resident, "Jesus loves you."

The residents and staff always plead, "Won't you please come back soon?"

On the way home after a performance, our group would discuss the visit, compare stories and enjoy the results of the day. Our feelings were the same every time. We were blessed as much as those we had visited.

TEACHING CHILDREN TO MINISTER

This kind of program offers tremendous possibilities to choir directors and youth departments. In most churches, the choir director works for months to teach children a musical presentation. Then, after one church performance, the children begin learning new songs. Wouldn't it be wonderful if the presentation at church was called a dress rehearsal? The real performances would be the ones in the community's long-term care facilities. How thrilling, for these elderly shut-ins, to see children and hear them sing!

Equally as important, however, is the impact made on the children. It is ideal. The church first teaches the children about service, then provides a tangible way to serve the Lord.

Volunteers who will gather the wheelchair residents and wheel them into the services are a vital part of all group activities. Many residents love to go to any activity offered. Others are capable of attending but are hesitant to venture out of the perceived security of their rooms. Often, with a bit of encouragement, they will attend these gatherings.

2. IMPROMPTU VISITING

Programs and activities mean a great deal to residents in professional care homes. Some Christians are ministering, but more help is needed to service the homes devoid of Christian programs. However, in spite of the effectiveness of these groups, another segment of oldsters remains virtually unnoticed. Among forgotten seniors exists an "inner group" of people not being reached.

The head nurse of an eighty-bed facility estimated that, "about one-third of skilled nursing care residents never leave their rooms! Of these people, half are bedridden and can't go out, and the other half are afraid to leave their rooms." I asked this nurse how many volunteers in her facility visited the room-bound patients.

She thought for a moment, "A couple of times a woman dressed like a clown came here, did tricks and told jokes. She went from room-to-room."

"What about the church groups that come?" I inquired. "Don't they go into the rooms to see the people who can't come to their services?"

"Well, no," she replied. "They give their program, shake a few hands and leave. I'm not criticizing them. I'm grateful they come at all. I only wish they had time to cheer up some of my people who can't come to the services." Although a few church groups reach out to the isolated individuals, most room-bound patients are forgotten by the Christian community. Maybe this is where God could use you the most. Perhaps you, as an individual Christian, could go into these rooms and show these people that they are loved!

Impromptu visiting can be done with other volunteers or perhaps you will feel led to venture out on your own. Some years, I had a day and time set aside to visit and other times, I went when I could. When an hour or so became available, I grabbed the time and went to visit nursing home occupants. Occasionally, a friend would accompany me but more often, I'd go alone (but of course, never without the Lord). Sometimes our family-owned business slowed down which allowed more time for visiting.

God has given me some special experiences. One such day (I'll treasure it forever,) began when I walked down a retirement home hallway. A lady tapped my shoulder and asked if I could sing a song for her. "Sure," I said, and strumming on my autoharp, I started singing.

She knew the hymn and began to sing along with me. Before the song ended, wonderful old ladies and men appeared from their rooms up and down the hall. We soon had about twenty singers gathered in this spontaneous sing-along. We sang and sang. No sooner would we finish the last verse of one song than someone would say, "How about *Amazing Grace*," or "How about *How Great Thou Art?*" If I didn't know the right chords, we just sang a cappella.

For about forty-five minutes, we all felt as if we were part of a heavenly chorus singing praises to our Lord. It was a moment in time that just happened. The privilege of seeing the glow on the faces of these saints of the Lord as they sang praises to Him, made the concerns of this world pale in importance.

The discovery of the needs and rewards of rest-home visiting began in my life about seventeen years ago.

My ninety-year-old grandmother died in a nursing home. At that time, my mother became aware of the loneliness in these professional care homes. The needs she observed and the grief she felt from losing her mom, prompted her to action.

She embarked on a mission of visiting the elderly. She and my mother-in-law, both shy, unassuming women who love the Lord, contacted a local nursing home. They asked the administration if any residents had no family or friends. This began their simple one-on-one ministry. These loving volunteers continued visiting for a number of years. Because of the faithfulness of these two ladies, and the Christmas "box-house", I finally entered a nursing home. My ministry as a volunteer began.

There have been seasons when visiting was not possible. During my last pregnancy and the illness and home going of both my parents, I stopped visiting altogether. Each time though, the Lord renewed me. I was able to return to see old friends "inside" and again meet new, wonderful people.

For most of us there are times of physical or emotional drain when we need members of the Christian community to minister to our needs. Then in time, the Lord enables us to go back out and serve him by helping others.

Be original. Explore different ways of ministering. Here are suggestions to assist your impromptu room-to-room visits:

a. Gifts.

You may feel most comfortable meeting people and presenting small gifts to them. Those who are able to read greatly appreciate good Christian books. Many books are available in large print editions.

A Shepherd Looks at the 23rd Psalm by Phillip Keller is a splendid present for both Christians and non-Christians. Nearly everyone seems to love the 23rd Psalm. This book presents the gospel as well as comforting and teaching believers.

Large print Bibles or New Testaments make wonderful gifts. Contact Gideons International about their policies for giving out free giant-print New Testaments.

Many residents love receiving flowering plants. Since plants need watering and care, you have a convenient excuse to return regularly to visit. Set the plant inside a handmade container inscribed with a Bible verse. The Word of God will provide comfort in time of affliction.[27]

One enterprising lady that I heard about through Love Thy Neighbor Ministries,[28] makes red and green Christmas stockings. The red ones are for the ladies and the green for the men. She gathers gifts (many from local merchants) such as combs, perfume, aftershave, handkerchiefs and soap. One year she provided two hundred of these "custom" gift stockings to a local nursing home.

Until you become a seasoned visitor, do not bring things to patients that are not first checked out by the staff. There is no need to ask about literature or greeting cards. During my father's residency in a convalescent hospital, God taught me an valuable lesson about giving.

Christmas was nearing, and I wanted to give him a gift, but he didn't need anything. He owned more "stuff" than his portion of the room could hold so most of his belongings were in storage. The need was mine. I wanted to give at Christmas.

After prayer, the Lord showed me that my father would also love to be able to give at Christmas time. A week before Christmas, I gave him two presents. One was a box of wooden tree ornaments and the was other a large tin of cookies. He opened the box of ornaments and a puzzled look came on his face. He hesitatingly said, "Well, thank you honey."

I smiled. "Daddy, you said the nurses in here were so nice to you. I thought you might like to give them a Christmas present!"

The look of appreciation on my dad's face was all I needed that year for Christmas. Handing out those ornaments and cookies was just what he needed, too.

Select gifts that can be given in turn to other residents or staff. Items such as whole boxes of assorted greeting cards, bookmarks, Christmas tree ornaments or decorative hair combs are suitable. The nursing home environment does not offer many opportunities for the residents to give to others. They love you for giving them the chance to once again be the giver.

Moving into a group home is a frustrating experience to most patients. Residents must adjust to being served by others. Personal freedoms and the rewarding feeling of helping others have been taken away. Imagine being uprooted from your residence and moved into an unfamiliar room already occupied by several strangers. In addition to this trauma, there is the unspoken knowledge that you are no longer needed and this may be your last earthly home.

Some well-meaning relatives try to tell the family member that this home experience is only temporary. Usually all parties know in their hearts that this is not actually the case. Again, remember to bring little gifts the residents can distribute to their roommates and the staff. This giving to others can return some of the self-esteem lost through aging and the nursing home experience.

b. Music.

Singing or playing any portable instrument provides an entree into a new room. Often the resident will ask for a favorite song or join you in familiar ones. I usually sing Christian songs. The songs of the world, however enjoyable, do not tell of eternal hope and truth. Just as we daily choose to spend time either on temporary or on everlasting projects, so our visit can bring temporary levity or eternal values to mind.

c. Listening.

Much of our life is spent listening. It is probably the most wonderful talent you possess! Use it in a nursing home. Listening, real listening, is a scarce commodity that is very meaningful to the residents. Listening says, "I care about you as a person." Not only will your visits be appreciated as you give genuine attention to their thoughts, you will also be opening the door to possible spiritual discussions.

d. Talking and Touching.

Conversations with the residents are easy to begin, and as you gain experience they become an art form. Holding hands, applying hand lotion or rubbing a back are special touches of love. If you feel unsure of proper topics for conversation, the next chapter offers many suggestions.

Make sure you know how to witness. Many of the residents have little time left to prepare for their everlasting destination. We need to use our time wisely. I still remember, many years ago, first hearing this concept being preached...

"Redeem the time the Bible says."[29] Our pastor spoke louder. "God is warning you that life is short. No matter how old you are, witness to others about Jesus Christ while you have the chance."

As a young Christian, this principle prompted me to prepare for witnessing. I studied so in case anyone asked how to become a Christian, I would be ready to answer. Unfortunately, as time passed by, I realized that people just didn't walk up and inquire, "Oh please, can you tell me how to become a Christian?" Consequently, I never told anyone.

As I searched the Bible, it became apparent to me that in most instances when Jesus spoke to people about knowing God, He spoke about a tangible object or principle that they understood. Then, with complete honesty and comfort, He related the familiar subject to knowing God. I began to understand the true nature of witnessing. In the natural course of a conversation, I could initiate a discussion about God's message. I remember discussing this concept in a Bible Study group when one of the high school girls said, "Sure, but what do you actually say?"

Her voice dropped off, "I really want to tell my friends about Jesus, but I don't know what to say and I don't know if they want to listen to me."

She certainly echoed my earlier feelings as a Christian. I was bound by protocol. My concern about waiting for the perfect time to speak caused countless, good opportunities to slip by.

I asked the teenager, "You have a new horse, right?"

"Yes," she smiled.

"Do any of your friends ride or have any interest in horses?"

"No, not that I know of," she replied.

"But have you told any of them about your new horse?" I urged.

"Oh, yes," she bubbled. "They've all heard about him. I can't stop talking about him."

I explained, "We have trouble finding 'opportunities' to witness because we actually are not being honest in our contacts with people. We love Jesus and pray daily about the details of our lives and then we are afraid to speak about God as a real person with whom we're involved. In our everyday encounters, we hold back and are afraid to speak of Him. We are more concerned about offending a fellow human being than we are about telling others of our eternal Savior."

The teenager began to see how natural witnessing should be. Your "honesty-in-witnessing" could begin by mentioning to people, other than your Christian friends, that God answered your prayers in a special way. Tell the details with enthusiasm. You may tell about something terrific you discovered in the Bible or relate a testimony you've just heard. If God is real to you, then **not** speaking of him should be difficult. As you learn to naturally speak to other people about God, you will enjoy your daily walk with Him even more.

Of course you'll discover that some people will not be at all interested in your story (at least they act that way). Others, however, will surprise you and finally, as you wished all along, they will actually ask you to tell them about Jesus.

Whenever you are able to talk to the elderly about God, don't be afraid to be direct. Ask them if they know Jesus personally. Because of your own religious upbringing you may prefer to use "saved", "born again", "converted", "had an experience", or another term that is comfortable. Be careful, though, not to be too general so as not to offend. Many people would love to say, "Oh, yes, I believe in God," and hope that will satisfy both you and God. Remember the Bible says, *"Thou believest that there is one God; thou doest well: the devils also believe and tremble."*[30]

Countless numbers of so-called religious people who "believe in God" have never understood that an individual, personal commitment to God through Jesus Christ is necessary to become a child of God and to spend eternity with Him in heaven. Nothing less. Nothing more. Remember, even well-educated people who have lived many more years than you have, still might not understand the gospel of Jesus Christ.

Preparation for witnessing is mandated by God in I Peter 3:15. He says to always be prepared to give an answer to everyone who asks you and to also be able to give the reason for the hope that you have. However, preparation alone is not enough. We must learn to be honest and speak of Jesus to those we contact in our everyday lives.

e. Tapes and Reading.

If you're not a verbal person, then a great way to reach out is to offer to read from the Bible. Many bedridden patients love listening to teaching or gospel song tapes. Often patients are not able to use their arthritic hands to turn on a bedside radio. You can bring a portable recorder with you but leaving it overnight is not advisable. Items, even of a small monetary value, sometimes disappear in these homes so don't leave anything that you cannot afford to lose.

f. Show and Tell.

Bring in interesting items or pictures. These are useful conversation starters and residents love news from the outside.

Some homes even allow cats and dogs to visit. Animals can be useful conversation pieces and icebreakers in difficult situations. These furry visitors bring back memories of beloved pets. The residents love the opportunity to stroke a pet once again. Bringing in animals should be done only with specific permission from the home's director.

3. INVOLVING OTHERS

a. Organizing Volunteers.

Although you would love to befriend and reach out to the elderly, your gifts might lean more toward organizing than in interacting directly with people. That is wonderful. Organizational skills are essential for recruiting and equipping volunteers.

Try setting up a **pen pal** system between younger members of your local church and elderly residents. Many teenagers don't have transportation available, but they love to write. Young Christian housewives who can't arrange to visit might love to be a friend by mail.

Why not involve your church in an adopt-a-grandparent program? For one moment, imagine your feelings if you had outlived or had been abandoned by your family? Many residents have no one who cares about them personally. Can't you just see a grandmother's delight as she opens a birthday card from her new "family"?

Envision her smile as she fondles a homemade valentine decorated by an adopted grandchild. These personal touches mean more than you might imagine.

The feelings expressed by Katherine, a sweet, white-haired woman, showed me this. In spite of her confinement in a wheelchair because of a broken hip, her attitude was cheerful.

"Oh, I just love to see the children. There was this one little feller, cute as a bug, that came in with a group to sing Christmas carols to us. After they sang, this little tyke came over to me with a card in his hand. It was handmade. I think he made it." Katherine laughed as she remembered.

"Well, I don't think he really wanted to part with it. But he finally did and it was so nice. I kept that card up on my wall for weeks. Wasn't that nice of him to do that for me?"

Yes, it was nice. It was also nice of the parents and leaders who used their time and energy organize the visit.

Say! How about **adopt-a-friend**? Just think about all those retired people at church. Because they no longer contribute in the work force, they are unsure of their purpose in life. They just sit in front of a television set, believing they have nothing of value to offer anyone. What could be of more value than being a friend to a lonely shut-in, sharing God's message of love?

To generate interest in these adoption programs, try to interest the prospective "adopter" in a specific oldster. Take snapshots of residents who need company. Survey the residents. Find out their past hobbies, areas they've lived, education, past occupations and any other profile information. Use the pictures and survey information to interest outsiders in coming to meet residents.

Holidays are an ideal time to stir interest in the needs of the elderly. On most holidays, particularly Christmas, peoples' thoughts center on family activities and sharing with others. Why not make good use of these feelings and suggest a "Family Christmas Party"? Begin by painting a verbal picture of lonely grandmothers and grandfathers who will have no family to celebrate with this year. Then explain that the party will be held at a local nursing home!

Now, bring out the "pièce de résistance." Display a Christmas tree or another appropriate decoration that is gaily festooned with special ornaments. Each ornament lists the name, description and snapshot of a nursing home resident. If you decide to provide gifts for each "grandparent", be sure to consult social services for an list of appropriate items. On each ornament, include a suggested personalized gift selected from this list.

During a regular church service, invite every family to come forward, select a decoration and adopt their very own "Christmas grandparent". A weekend after-noon is the best time for your party. It's impractical to plan evening activities since patients usually go to bed quite early. To preserve the dignity of these special older citizens, make sure the people who help you at the party can identify the patients by name. This will enable the adoptive "grandparent" to be respectfully in-troduced to their new "relative".

Your party activities may include singing Christmas carols together and visual, funny games. You might finish the party with a dramatic presentation of The Nativity. Use your imagination and include some of the patients in the drama. The most important part of the afternoon is the family's special interest in their new family member.

A week following the party, suggest to the families who adopted, that it would be nice to keep up the con-tact with visits and letters. You might suggest, "It's a long time until next Christmas, and who knows if all of our new grandparents will still be around by then."

Families whose schedules don't allow them to par-ticipate in the party should be encouraged to adopt an oldster who is bedridden and was unable to attend the party.

b. Group Drop-In.

Involve your Sunday School class, Christian friends, teenage Sunday School classes, or your family

A unique aspect of this ministry is the broad age span of people that can be involved. Anyone, from infants to elderly, can delight these forgotten ones. I personally have known visitors from three months of age to eighty-five years old. From infancy, both of my children have joined in visiting. The residents delight to see and touch young children. The depth of understanding about aging and death my children gained was immeasurable. One afternoon when my daughter Rachel was five years old, we were visiting from room to room. We stopped at the first bed in a room to visit a new friend named Fred. After we chatted for a few minutes, Rachel offered to sing a song accompanying herself on a small harp.

As soon as she gaily began to sing "Jesus loves me, this I know," an angry voice from the other bed yelled out, "Who is that? What's that noise?" A curtain was drawn between the two beds so we couldn't see the irate person. I guessed from the voices on the other side that several attendants were helping a patient dress.

Rachel was undaunted by the interruption. She continued: "For the Bible tells me so." The man's angry voice continued to shriek through the curtain, "Stop that noise! Stop it right now!"

Fred was visibly touched by Rachel's song. As she sang, I silently prayed that she would not be scared. Seemingly undaunted, she completed the whole song. As she finished, the curtain was drawn aside. An attendant began wheeling the angry resident past us on the way out to the hallway. As the wheelchair passed by, the patient lashed out with his arm to hit Rachel, narrowly missing her.

the way out to the hallway. As the wheelchair passed by, the patient lashed out with his arm to hit Rachel, narrowly missing her.

Hoping this attack would not permanently frighten her, I quickly knelt down to her level, "Are you okay?"

She looked at me sadly, "Oh, Mom, I'll bet if he knew Jesus, he wouldn't act like that." Sometimes the vision of a child is so much clearer than that of an adult!

Recently a chance reunion with a young woman substantiated again the value of involving children. While she was a teenager, I had instructed her in horseback riding. After exchanging greetings, I mentioned that I was currently writing about visiting the elderly.

"I want to encourage others to participate in a visiting ministry," I explained.

She commented, "Don't you remember I went with you a couple of times?"

"Oh yes! You did, didn't you," I responded.

"It really wasn't my thing though," she added.

"Oh," I apologized, "I'm sorry. I know that it's not for everyone. I was so enthusiastic, I'm afraid, that all of you were pushed into my projects."

She quickly explained, "Oh, no, you don't understand. I'm glad you took me. You see, just a few years ago we had to make a decision to place my grandmother in a home. We couldn't handle her medical problems at home any more, but the rest of my family was afraid of those places. Because I had been inside a nursing home with you and seen that it was okay, I was able to reassure my family that we needed help and that the home would lovingly care for her."

If you would like to visit but don't feel ready to go alone, ask your own church about its visiting program. Inquire at a local nursing home to see if any Christians presently come to their establishment. If so, perhaps you could join with them. Some facilities I've visited provide information and suggestions for volunteer service.

Just as our standard of living often isolates us from the needs of people in abject poverty, so we are separated from the natural progression of aging and death. How sad that we keep so distant from these arenas of life. In so doing, we forfeit blessings and are not obeying God's Word because we fail to assist those in need. We also are failing to gain understanding for a future time when we may have to cope with the placement of one of our own aging loved ones.

Chapter 7

GETTING STARTED

"Okay, I'll go! What do I do now?"

First, study God's Word. Later in the book, you'll find lots of helpful verses to encourage and prepare you to visit. Other verses, selected especially for elderly residents, will assist you as you visit.

Second, pray for wisdom and guidance. God says,

"If any of you lack wisdom let him ask of God, that giveth to all men liberally, and upbraideth not." [31]

God never says, "That was a dumb question." You can also glean information from the later chapters which relate stories of actual visits.

Third, remember the many programs described in the previous chapters. Select one of these or use another one that God would reveal to you. Put your "gift" in operation.

Fourth, set aside a time. Make it happen! If this is really God's will for you, then Satan will seek to detour you any way he can.

Fifth, go to the home you've selected. Before entering claim a victory for Jesus. Recognize that you are in the army of the Lord of Hosts. Remember God's words,

> *"Have not I commanded thee? Be strong and of good courage; be not afraid, neither be thou dismayed; for the Lord thy God is with thee whithersoever thou goest."* [32]

Sixth, go in and ask permission to visit from the social director, head nurse, office manager or whoever seems to be in charge. Claim God's promise,

> *"Be strong and of a good courage, fear not; nor be afraid of them: for the Lord thy God, he it is that doth go with thee; he will not fail thee, nor forsake thee."* [33]

Recently, incidents of robbery and molestation have surfaced in professional care homes. If you are a man going into a new nursing home, you may elect to be accompanied by several volunteers. Since visitation ministries are uncommon, particularly among men, the accompanying people should allay any fear the staff may feel. God tells us to *"Abstain from all appearance of evil."* [34]

After you have established yourself as a trustworthy volunteer, you can then feel free to minister individually to both men and women. This group beginning is not a must. Pray for wisdom in the specifics of your own ministry.

Seventh, if God is really who you say He is, then believe Him for a fruitful ministry.

The Bible says,

"Delight thyself also in the Lord; and he shall give thee the desires of thine heart." [35]

This is an appropriate number to conclude this plan as seven signifies completion and rest.

Chapter 8

ROOM ETIQUETTE

You have received permission to visit, yet here you stand in the hallway. How do you enter a room for the first time?

HOW TO ENTER A ROOM

It is essential to keep in mind that this is the occupant's home - the last space they can call their own.

Don't barge in. Imagine yourself as a guest, visiting in the resident's home. This is a considerate approach. Unfortunately, staff members must enter without invitation, simply because of their workload or the resident's condition. Some homes have the resident's names on the doors or beds. This is very useful. You might make a written note of names until you can remember unassisted.

Most of the seniors come from a more formal era than ours today. Because of this, be careful about using a new acquaintance's first name without being asked to do so. Usually when you say, "Excuse me, what is your name?" they respond with their last name. You will sense in most cases when it is proper to ask if you can call them by their first name.

Although this procedure may seem too formal to some volunteers, the importance of this and other social graces is immense. These courtesies will give back to these institutionalized seniors a measure of dignity.

Before entering, softly rap on the door frame and ask permission to come in. Most of the time you will not be heard from the hallway. It is then acceptable to step through the doorway with a soft friendly greeting. Try to avoid startling anyone. Continue to talk until your greeting is acknowledged. The warmth of your voice can reassure the resident. Many of these people are hard of hearing or semi-blind. Always move slowly and speak softly at first to avoid startling the occupants of the room.

A typical greeting could be, "Hello, may I come in?" or, "Hello, my name is . . .." Maintain, if possible, an atmosphere in which the resident remains the host or hostess, and you the invited guest.

Often, even a return visit goes smoother if you will mention your name as you enter. This saves possible embarrassment for the resident. Sometimes they won't remember your name. Others will not even recall that you have visited them before. It's not that you are un-wanted. Even those residents who forget, still appreciate your visit at the time.

Speaking of forgetfulness and return visits, you may also need some help. After a day of visiting, jot down notes about some of the conversations you had. These notes will be very helpful on future visits. This information will help you demonstrate genuine interest in your new friend. It will also be reassuring to you.

Usually the residents recognize you and love your return visits. You'll receive friendly greetings from them such as, "Oh, you came back! Come on in. Sit down and visit awhile."

WORDS OF CAUTION

You must always knock and wait for an invitation before opening anyone's closed door.

Most rooms have curtains that can be drawn around the patients' beds for privacy. Respect these closed curtains. You must not peer behind them unless the resident calls for you or asks you to open the curtain.

Some residents may seem unfriendly and not want your company at first. Without being overbearing, try to convey your reason for being there. You might say, "I was here visiting and wondered if I could meet you?" Elderly people are often suspicious at first and if you state you are seeking to make new friends, it seems to alleviate their fears.

BEGINNING CONVERSATION

Avoid the standard American conversation opener, "Hi, how are you today?" In our culture this greeting is as natural as breathing. In the nursing home environment, however, this salutation should be discarded. Many residents are neither well nor happy, and you open a Pandora's box if you use it. On subsequent visits when you're better acquainted, use this greeting with discernment.

A more acceptable conversation opener can be discovered by glancing around to locate something distinctive about the residents or their rooms. Look for anything unique. Try a remark about wallpaper or furniture. Observe their clothes, hair style, jewelry or displayed memorabilia.

These conversations about weather, memorabilia or room decorations are the easiest to sustain. It is usually best to avoid discussing ailments. The residents have many physical disorders and dwelling on negatives can be depressing. It is better to guide the conversation to those faculties that are still working well. Smile. Be cheerful. You've come to bring love and hope. Apply the scripture that says, *"A merry heart doeth good like a medicine."* [36]

People tend to lose their individuality in an institution, so it gives their egos a boost when you find something attractive about them or their "homes". Don't patronize; be genuine. Love them and they will love in return.

Try to observe any praiseworthy actions. They appreciate praise. It will help their sense of personal value, which is difficult to maintain in an institutional environment.

When one person does not want company, you may still visit another in the same room. Excuse yourself to the one and say, "Perhaps we can visit another time" (or something to this effect). Many times you will find people who are slow to warm up to you but, in time, will love your company.

ENCOURAGEMENT

Talking about the fact that we are spiritual beings inside of a physical body is usually well received. Sometimes you'll meet Christians who believe they would be better off dead because they feel useless and a burden to those around them. It is a privilege to share scriptures with those people that show the perfection of God's timing. Point out that they live in a mission field.

You could tell them that many people (staff and patients) need their friendship and prayers. Suggest, "Perhaps this is a special quiet time in your life when you can pray for the needs of others." Remember you are not merely applying good bedside manners; this is the truth.

Often a song or conversation will bring tears to the eyes of the elderly as they recall a departed loved one. You may comment, "You must have really loved him," or, "Tell me something about her." They then will recall happy times and their faces will brighten. To lonely widows and widowers who are Christians, you may speak in glowing terms of reunions in heaven. Many of these people are not far from being with the Lord. You will both be blessed by speaking of the joys of heaven. Then bring them back to the present. Mention that God has definite purposes in allowing some to go ahead to be with him and others to stay behind. Help them discover those purposes through scriptures and discussion.

CONFUSION

Sometimes residents make statements that obviously are not true. You may be told, "My mother is coming to see me today," or "I've got to go weed my garden." Resist correcting them by saying, "What you've just said cannot be right, your mother must be dead." Instead, gently probe for the feelings behind their statements. You could reply, "Do you miss your mom?" or "Could I be your friend today?" It's usually a feeling that the elderly residents are expressing in their obviously unreal statements.

Realize that you are visiting to share the love the Lord has given you through Jesus Christ. Do it!

For many who cannot understand or hear your words, a touch and a smile are important. Never hesitate to give these gestures of kindness even though you receive no sign of recognition in return.

If individuals can not tell you their names after you introduce yourself, gently pick up their wrist and read the arm band. People love to hear their own names. To some who struggle to speak but cannot, gently suggest that God understands their thoughts. Encourage them to speak to Him because, "He loves you very much."

ON THE JOB TRAINING

Many times while visiting, the Lord has given me "on the job training". I will never forget the lessons learned during one day of visiting . . .

"Mama, I'm excited! This one's going to be great. I just know it." My perky blond daughter beamed with anticipation as she slid out of the front seat of our car.

"Now Rachel," I said, "you can't always tell by an attractive building what the people inside will be like. Remember a couple of times we met people who weren't too friendly."

We walked toward the front entrance, wondering just what kind of place it would be. It certainly appeared pleasant from the outside. The sign in front read, "Colonial Manor-Skilled Nursing Care." Tall white columns matched the name while the neatly tended purple and yellow petunias beside the lawn suggested friendliness.

Once inside, we were pleased to see lots of bright colors in the wallpaper, clothes, and accessories of the elderly residents. We decided our day was going to be special when several patients wheeled over to us with smiles on their faces. So often older people are drawn to Rachel. They appear to appreciate the opportunity to speak and to touch a child. After chatting, hugging and singing a few familiar hymns, we began our room-to-room exploration. I say exploration, because we never quite know what to expect as we enter a room.

At room 12, we received permission from the occupant of the first bed to enter and visit. I introduced myself and asked if she would like to hear a song today. The lady, who identified herself as Maudie, said, "Oh, yes, I'd love that." I began to strum my autoharp and launched into singing *The Old Rugged Cross*. As I sang, Maudie joined in eagerly, hardly missing a single word.

During the singing, Rachel slipped over to the bed of the second occupant of the room, intending to hold hands with her. Rachel, a second grader, was still somewhat shy. It surprised me then to hear her initiate conversation with the prone elderly woman. She leaned down to her new friend and gently inquired, "What is your name?"

The lady grabbed her hand and said, "We-We."

Rachel seemed puzzled but asked again, "What is your name?"

The woman once more responded with an urgent, "We-We."

At that moment all kinds of thoughts tumbled in my mind as I continued singing with Maudie. My concern was how Rachel would react to this unintelligible answer. I was afraid this woman's strange reply would squelch further bravery in Rachel.

This may have been an overreaction, but I can't envision any mother being at ease while her second-grader's hand is held captive by an unfamiliar elderly woman who continues to urge, "We-We! We-We!"

Upon concluding the song, I quickly moved to the second bed to rescue Rachel. I suggested to Rachel, "Maybe she only speaks French. 'Oui Oui' is yes yes in French."

On this hunch, I tried speaking some of my high school French to the lady, but she didn't seem to understand. Then I whispered to Rachel, "Maybe this woman is like some of the others we have met that are just very confused." "Perhaps," I thought to myself, "the lady really does need to go to the bathroom, or maybe it is just her feeble way of gaining attention." I assumed it was one of these possibilities until I began slipping Rachel's hand from the lady's firm hold. Trying to be polite, I said, "Maybe we could come back again some time and sing to you."

She then grabbed my hand, looked deeply into my eyes, and said, "Oh, WEEE, we we, WE, we, we, we, weee!" I began to realize that Rachel's apparent calmness during the confusing conversation was based on a communication that goes far beyond spoken language.

After singing several more hymns in this room, we said our goodbye's and headed straight for the nurse's station to solve the mystery of our "we-we" lady.

"Oh, yes," the head nurse replied to our question, "that's Mary in 12-b. She had a stroke two years ago. She understands everything when you talk to her, but she can only speak the word 'we'. She's a very bright lady - been all over the world, and loves the Lord very much."

Then our unusual encounter made perfect sense. Mary was simply overjoyed at the unexpected Christian fellowship and the love of God expressed through the touch of a child. Rachel and I have had many deep conversations since that day, based on our newfound friend. Subsequent visits with Mary have demonstrated to both of us how important it is to know God through Jesus Christ. Mary is locked inside a prison more effective than bars and walls, and yet the peace we've seen in her eyes, her smile, the squeeze of her hand and the expression in her voice are witness to a human spirit totally submitted to God.

People who have had strokes often lose the ability to express their thoughts in words. This condition is called "expressive aphasia". As you might imagine, this is an extremely frustrating situation for the patient.

Whenever you meet a resident who seems alert but continues to repeat the same words over and over, you may have encountered a stroke victim. If this is verified by an attendant, you must be especially thoughtful and perceptive. These patients can communicate through their eyes and hand squeezes and also by the tone and inflection of their repeated words. If given opportunity, they sometimes can write their thoughts.

CREATING FRIENDLY VISITS

When you visit a resident in their room, always ask permission before sitting in a chair or on a bed. This maintains the sensation that you consider yourself "company" in their home.

Try to position yourself on the same eye level as the person you visit. This has importance. Standing above a person when you speak implies authority and weakens the self esteem of the other person. If you sit or kneel, the resident tends to relax and enjoy your presence much more. I have even knelt by a wheelchair resident so that my eye level was lower than their eye level. This produces a sense of confidence in a patient.

Sometimes the phrase "I'd like to visit with you (or sing a song for you) if you have time" is very useful. This question will bring mirth to the rational, since they have time in abundance. The partly senile patients will be humored. They ponder your question a moment to decide whether or not they have time and then invite you in.

Some residents like to hear about your life and what is going on in the outside world. Others enjoy reminiscing and telling you about their past. If you are sensitive and listen well, you will know what to say. Remember, just listening to a person says, "Because I feel you are important, I want to hear what you have to say."

AVOIDING MISTAKES

Do not change anything in the room, such as the bed, light or window position. Adjusting covers is acceptable, but any other changes should be done by the staff. A startling reminder of the danger of unthinking volunteers scared me one day.

A friend and I arrived at a nursing home on an impromptu visit. As we strode toward the front entrance, we panicked at the sight of an elderly lady in a wheelchair headed for disaster. The custom of many wheelchair patients is to roll themselves to doorways to watch and wait. This home had a cement porch reached by a number of steps. The sweet elderly lady had forgotten what steps were and was oblivious to what would happen to her when she rolled off the porch.

We ran forward and grabbed her chair just inches before she would have toppled to disaster. We trembled, praising the Lord for His timing in enabling us to rescue her.

Later we discovered that a gentleman had just entered the front door to visit a relative. This lady had asked him, "Please, will you hold the door open so I can roll my wheelchair outside?" Unfortunately, not sensing the danger, he had complied and then walked on inside. We were overwhelmed at how easily a kind, but uninformed gesture could cause a disaster.

Another misguided act of kindness occurred when a polite old gentleman asked if I could please unbutton the cuffs on his flannel shirt sleeves. "Please, help me with these ma'am. They're too tight and I can't get them undone." I hesitated, but observing his arthritic hands and sensing no harm, complied. He became Houdini. Within seconds, he had taken off both his flannel shirt and his undershirt. Only then did I realize that the buttoned cuffs kept him from disrobing his upper body. Sheepishly, I approached a nurse and had to ask her to replace his clothes.

FORGETFULNESS

Just because residents forget who you are (or even who they are) is never an excuse to betray their trust. Be careful not to make promises that you cannot keep. As you visit it's so easy to be caught up in the joy of the moment. You'll find yourself promising these appreciative oldsters that you will come back soon. Don't say it if you don't mean it!

Short, frequent visits are better than occasional, long ones. Residents tire easily and often have limited attention spans.

Long-term memory of the elderly is more reliable than short-term. This accounts for the residents being able to wax eloquent on their past life but yet be unable to remember their own room number. Eventually, you learn not to be surprised when the often-visited resident says, "Who are you? Have we ever met before?" You will hear the same stories told over and over and over. This can be a real test of your love and patience. Listen to the often-repeated story as if it's the first time you heard it.

Always assume, as you meet new residents, that they possess all their mental facilities. Give yourself time to get acquainted. Sometimes, you will discover people who seemed slow mentally were just shy or introverted.

NOT EVERYONE IS ATTRACTIVE

Most of the elderly you meet are fun and interesting company. However, you will meet people

who, because of physical breakdowns, are definitely
not pleasant to the eye. They may be missing limbs,
have become incontinent or have other unpleasant body
disorders. You may not be at all comfortable with such
people. Try to remember their body is just the house in
which they live. Look beyond what you see with your
physical eyes. God tells us, *"Though our outward man
perish, yet the inward man is renewed day by day."* [37]

If you feel repulsed, pray to have the heart and eyes
of Jesus. He even saw lepers as people to care for and
love. It may take time. Be patient with yourself - God
is. If you can't yet reach out to these unsightly few,
then smile and move on but never register distaste.
They're already hurting inside so don't add to their discomfort.

Others will appear unreachable and unfriendly.
Don't reject them by passing without at least attempt-
ing a gesture of friendliness. Ignoring their existence
only drives them deeper into the solitude of rejection.

PHYSICAL BREAKDOWN

Occasionally residents will comment, "It's so dark in
here. Why don't they turn more lights on?" This question may surprise you as the lighting seems just fine.
The reason they want more light is that they are
gradually losing their eyesight, possibly from
cataracts.

Usually I try to be agreeable and make honest but
general comments such as, "The sun didn't come out
much today," or, "I know what you mean. A little more
light would be nice." There are reasons for this evasive
language. First, most patients do not live long enough
to become functionally blind so there is no reason to

add to their fear. Second, it's certainly not a volunteer's place to say, "You're going blind."

Be very cautious about suggesting buying hearing aids or glasses. Untimely ideas can upset the elderly. Frequently, valid reasons exist for the aids they do or do not possess.

PRACTICAL CONCERNS

It is helpful to know the residents' routines such as mealtimes and activities scheduled by the home. Older people do not like changes. You should learn to work around the established routines of their lives.

Most homes have smoking areas. These patio and alcove gatherings are convenient places to begin conversations. However, nonsmokers may find it uncomfortable as the smoke becomes rather thick at times.

Wear bright colors and patterns when possible; the residents appreciate your cheerful appearance. Also, if you are a woman and have long hair, wear it down. Most of these ladies once had flowing tresses, but not any more. Their hair is cut because they are too old to take care of it any more. They miss their ancient symbol of womanhood and love to touch yours.

A word of caution. When you have a cold or flu, stay home! Resistance to illness is low in the elderly so your sniffles could develop into their pneumonia. Remember to faithfully wash your hands before and after visiting.

SPIRITUAL CONVERSATIONS

It is usually evident when you enter a room whether or not people are believers. After a little practice, it becomes easy to visit and share Christ with those who are not.

It is also noticeable in some rooms that a bad spirit is present. Satan sometimes has people convinced that he permanently owns them. Don't you believe it. Jesus is the victor. Call on His strength. By faith in God's power, Satan will lose again.

Elderly people entertain serious thoughts about life and death and the meaning of their existence. Many enjoy discussing Jesus, the Lord and the purpose of life. They have had a lifetime of fillers and entertainment; now they want to discuss purpose and future.

Conversation about the Lord can begin by mentioning that you enjoy the company of people who have lived and seen a lot. Mention that many times you find people who have lived a few extra years probably know what is really important in life. At this point, genuine Christians will usually identify themselves, if they haven't already. Unbelievers will become evasive because, in fact, they haven't yet figured out the truth about life. You will discover some who prefer only to discuss their church. They do so because they have never established a personal relationship with God.

When you feel that your visit should end, stand up and say how much you enjoyed meeting and visiting with them. Also ask if you might come back again sometime. Some will try to pay you. You might reply in mock surprise, "I came in friendship and friendship is without price."

As you gain experience in ministering, you will
sense when touching a resident is appropriate. You
may decide to give a hug, a soft kiss on the cheek or
just squeeze their hand. Be gentle. They are fragile.

COORDINATING YOUR VISITS

It is a very rare occurrence to receive opposition
from hospital staff. Most of them are well aware of the
residents' needs for companionship.

The larger establishments have activity directors and
it is wise to know who they are. Any scheduled
program goes through them. Impromptu visits are
under the auspices of the management. Once you've
gained permission to enter a particular home, you are
usually welcome to visit at your convenience without
asking each time.

Try to minister to residents when relatives are not
likely to be there. Too many people in a room at one
time is confusing. It is better for the lonely ones if you
can fill in an empty day when they have no company. Residents' families and friends are most likely to
visit on holidays and weekends.

After you form a genuine friendship with someone,
it is worthwhile to meet their family. There is sometimes an opportunity to witness and encourage them
also. Consigning a loved one to a professional home
can be a stressful experience for the family.

After years of visiting in convalescent homes, it became necessary to find such a place for my own father.
Then I had my turn at being the visiting relative. I, too,
experienced the guilt, the sadness and the frustration of
having a beloved parent die away from home. During
his stay there, I experienced in a personal way, the

importance of outside people who enter and visit the residents during their twilight time on earth.

You may develop friendships with someone who has no friends or family. Try to acknowledge them on their birthdays and holiday. These days can be especially lonely for the residents when there is no contact from anyone on the outside.

Leaving your denominational Christian literature can be a real "put off" to residents or their relatives who are of another faith. When selecting written material, choose good Christian literature not identified with a particular group. Avoid "anti" tracts or "Are you ready to die?" pamphlets. Don't rely on a piece of paper to replace the Holy Spirit's power to lead your conversation. Certainly the subject of death can be discussed. However, this sensitive yet crucial topic should be handled in-person, lovingly and one-on-one.

MOST IMPORTANT!

People love to feel that your motives for visiting them are personal not organizational. When people discover that you are not there representing a certain group or church but have come on your own they are surprised and impressed. They realize that you are actually interested in them as a person. When you do visit as part of a church group, try not to mention this too soon in conversation.

Also, with staff and family, try not to represent a particular church or denomination. Some people may reject spiritual discussion if your denomination is not the same as theirs. Instead, speak of knowing God through Jesus Christ our Savior.

Chapter 9

LOTS OF STORIES

Every visit produces a new story. Here are a few to give you insight into the worthwhile benefits of visiting.

CHILDLIKE FAITH

In one room, I discovered a beautiful grey-haired lady about eighty years old. She sat peacefully on her last piece of furniture, an overstuffed chair. She wore a lace-trimmed dress, and her dainty hands were folded neatly in her lap. Blue eyes sparkled behind unframed spectacles, and as I came near, she smiled. It took a lot of effort for her to speak; she seemed to have forgotten most of her vocabulary. This embarrassed her so she shook her head, "Go visit somebody else. Don't bother with me; I can't think very well."

I told her that I had lots of time and she mustn't worry if she couldn't quite remember everything. She seemed pleased when I suggested, "God understands you even when you don't speak a single word."

I asked her if she knew Jesus and my eyes widened upon her reply.

"I don't believe I've ever met Him."

I had the choice of going no further in witnessing because of her simple answer, or continuing. Since I know God made the gospel simple enough even for a child to understand, I continued. I explained how God loves us through Jesus and how we can belong to God's family through faith. She knit her brow, "I think I'd like that."

We prayed together and she told God that she wanted to trust in Jesus. Praise God for another miracle birth into his family!

ROOMMATE'S LOVE

One afternoon while walking down a hallway, a grey-haired lady wheeled her chair toward me. I smiled at her and she smiled in return. She glanced curiously at my autoharp, so I asked her if she would like to hear a song. "Yes," she replied, "that would be interesting."

After the hymn, she offered, "My name is Vera. Would you please come to my room and sing for my roommate? I know she will love it."

She led me to her room. I entered, and smiled at the woman in bed.

"Hello, my name is Dorothy. Would you like to hear a song today?"

"No! I'm in pain. I don't want anyone in here. Come back some other time."

Vera's face saddened as she gazed at her friend. She had so wanted to cheer her beloved roommate. Our faithful Lord again showed me how to handle a difficult situation.

"Oh, I'm sorry you're not feeling well. I had hoped to meet you. You know, sometimes music will soothe the pain. Do you suppose I could try just one short song? I'll sing real softly."

"Okay, if you want to, go ahead." After the song, she completely changed. She shared how God had twice saved her life and even now was dealing with her cancer. She asked for another song and we talked of God's provisions for us. As I was leaving she requested that I come to see her again soon.

The change in her feelings toward me resulted from the sincerity and love the Lord can give us if we let Him. Being able to meet people and to be sensitive to their real feelings is a Spirit-directed gift. The beauty of the Christian life is not that we are loving but that God allows us to be the channel of His love. The Bible says, *"No man hath seen God at any time"* but then wonderfully continues, *"If we love one another, God dwelleth in us, and his love is perfected in us."*[38]

A QUEEN

Cora appeared to be in her nineties. Wearing a plain white hospital gown, she lay flat under her bedcovers revealing only shriveled, gnarled arms. She looked at me but made no response as I spoke. I could find nothing physically attractive about her or her surroundings with which to begin a conversation. It wasn't even clear if she had the ability to understand me.

I checked the identification bracelet on her wrist in order to learn her name. Silver hair framed her face as her head nestled into the pillow, so I ventured, "Cora, your hair looks like a crown; it makes you look like a queen." Slowly, she moved one hand up and touched her hair. She reacted with a smile. I knew then she could understand me. I asked if I could sing a song to a queen. Faintly, she replied, "Yes." As the visit progressed, I was able to share Jesus with her through song and word.

About four weeks later, I visited her room again. Peeking around the corner, I smiled, "Cora, may I visit you today."

"No! Get out of here," she snapped. "The last time you brought me so much grief."

How is that for an opener? What would you do if you had just begun your ministry as a volunteer and received this kind of welcome? The natural response would be to wilt into the floor and slide out the door. In answer to a quick prayer and the leading of the Holy Spirit, the Lord gave me insight.

"Oh, Cora, I just remember what a nice visit we had together last time, and I was hoping we could do it again. Remember how we sang and how you looked like a queen?" Gradually she softened, and before long she was asking me to please sing one more song before I left.

RELUCTANT VISITOR

Cynthia, a beautiful blond girl of twenty-one recently returned to fellowship with the Lord. I mentioned the nursing home ministry in a conversation and she commented, "How nice, maybe I'll go with you sometime."

I volunteered, "It's possible that we could get together this Saturday."

"Well, I'll see," she replied. "Maybe it will work out."

Saturday came and the day's schedule opened up time for a visit. I had completely forgotten about asking Cynthia to go along. We lived on a busy horse ranch so there were always people on the premises. I prayed. "Lord, if there is someone who should go with me today, guide me to that person." I walked outside and there was Cynthia. She asked, rather disappointedly, "I suppose you're going visiting today?" She went on to explain that she really was afraid to go, didn't feel adequate and wanted to avoid going. The Lord had dealt with her all week. She finally responded, "Okay, I'll go to the ranch and if Dorothy is ready to go visit when I get there, I'll go. Otherwise, forget it."

Cynthia visited that day. Not only did the Lord minister greatly through her, but she continued to visit on her own after that. Faith, as small as a grain of mustard seed, overcame her reluctance. Jesus said,

> *"If ye have faith as a grain of a mustard seed, ye shall say unto this mountain, Remove hence to yonder place; and it shall remove; and nothing shall be impossible unto you."*[39]

NO GOOD FOR ANYTHING

One day, I entered a room occupied by three ladies. After chatting and singing with the first two, I made my way to the third lady, but before I could speak she said, "Go away. Don't bother with me. I can't hear and I can't see. Go see someone else." I asked her if I could just sit with her. She hesitated, then said," All right."

After a weary sigh, the despondent lady spoke. "My name is Marta. I come from Norway in 1920...I'm ninety-seven years old... I cannot see to read and I cannot hear anyone. I'm not good for anything...I wish God would let me die."

I tried to reassure her, but inside I was hurting because I didn't know how to minister to her. I was frustrated and I felt defeated. After leaving, I asked the Lord to please show me how to reach her.

Every time I visited, I would stop and sit with her. Conversing was difficult as Marta could barely hear even when I spoke loudly right into her ear.

On about the fifth visit, as I approached Marta, she reached out both arms toward me. With her engaging Norwegian accent she exclaimed, "Oh, Dor-tay Me-lur, my friend."

God answers prayer. Marta was reached not by clever words, but by the simplicity of God's love conveyed through a believer. On subsequent visits, we developed a communication system and I was able to share some promises from God's Word with her. If I miss seeing her for a few weeks, she says, "Oh, I taut perhaps you weren't going to come see me anymore." That kind of greeting haunts me when I get too busy in my work-a-day world to visit these new-found friends.

SHY GIRL CARES

Tami is a shy, insecure girl of fifteen. She loves the Lord but is not very forward in talking to strangers. She has known sorrow in her life through her parent's divorce and the early death of her mother. She possesses a sensitivity beyond her years. Anytime she has transportation to visit in the nursing homes, she goes. Often she will just smile, hold a hand, or say a few words. Most importantly, she goes and loves and cares. People feel this and appreciate her attention.

The Bible says,

> *"He which soweth sparingly shall reap also sparingly; and he which soweth bountifully shall reap also bountifully. Every man according as he purposeth in his heart, so let him give; not grudgingly, or of necessity: for God loveth a cheerful giver."* [40]

This passage teaches us how to give our money, but in Tami's life there are other commodities given - time and love.

SISTER'S REQUEST

While I was singing in a nursing home hallway one afternoon, a middle-aged lady came out of a nearby room. She asked, "Please, could you come in and sing to my sister, Dora? She has a brain tumor, and they've give her only a few weeks to live. She doesn't know us most of the time, but while you were singing she actually sang with you. She even knew all the words!"

That day, my friend Lorraine had come along for her first visit. I suggested she introduce herself to the other bedridden lady in the room while I sang to the dying woman. Sure enough, Dora sang along with every song. As she sang, her sister and brother-in-law stood beside the bed with tears streaming down their faces.

During the last hours of a loved one's life, the family wants desperately to show their love through some kindness. Often, however, there is very little to which the failing person will respond. Out of gratitude the brother-in-law offered, "Please, let me pay you." I was able to tell them of Jesus and the love God gives His children to share freely with others.

Meanwhile, Lorraine had encountered difficulty. Nell, the frail old lady she was visiting, was extremely disturbed. Her wrists were comfortably but firmly tied to the bed. She kept repeating, "Let me out of here. What have I ever done to you?" I tried to assist Lorraine in calming the distraught woman, but to no avail. Finally, we left the room feeling somewhat defeated.

We agreed that God had called us into that room. We saw how Dora and her family benefited from our visit. We kept assuring ourselves we couldn't expect to reach everyone. Still, Nell's complete despair and the sound of her wailing voice saying, "What have I ever done to you," played on our hearts. We prayed for her.

Later that week, I returned to visit Dora. After singing a hymn to her, I caught a glimpse of something out of the corner of my eye. I turned and saw Nell's two frail hands held in the air, above her head, silently clapping together. After each song, up came the hands in silent applause. I could hardly wait to go over to see her.

After concluding my visit with Dora, Nell's son entered and sat in a chair beside his mother's bed. I approached and spoke to Nell. "May I sing a song just for you?" She smiled in response.

Her well-meaning son said, "How about *'My Wild Irish Rose'*?" His mom's face instantly darkened and a frown appeared.

"Oh, I mostly just know hymns," I responded. "Would that be okay?"

He replied, "Whatever you do, go ahead."

I sang *The Old Rugged Cross*, after which Nell smiled and once again gave me the wonderful, silent, applause.

It was beautiful to see how God had quieted her spirit and given her peace through song. He was true to His Word.

"Yea, though I walk through the valley of the shadow of death, I will fear no evil: for thou art with me; thy rod and they staff they comfort me."[41]

Chapter 10

MORE STORIES - SURPRISING ADVENTURES

Occasionally, you will be totally rejected as you seek to minister to the elderly. There are various reasons people behave this way. They may be suspicious or fearful. These feelings often are a natural by-product of aging. These negative feelings are also produced by real or perceived disappointment in other people. Some residents are experiencing actual physical pain and wish to be alone. There also may be occasional times when people have strong anti-Christian feelings.

Since, apart from the Holy Spirit, you have no way to discern the particular reason for the rebuff, you need to appeal to God for wisdom. He may lead you to return another time, to leave the person alone altogether or to continue the visit right then.

If the visiting you do is serving God's purposes, then the resistance you encounter may be from Satan. Don't forget God says,

"Be sober, be vigilant; because your adversary the devil, as a roaring lion, walketh about, seeking whom he may devour." [42]

Satan may have a hold on some of the unresponsive patients, but we have access to a greater power . . . God's. This truth is clear throughout the Bible. It is specifically mentioned in such reassuring verses as,

"Ye are of God, little children, and have overcome them: because greater is he that is in you, than he that is in the world." [43]

Some strong reminders of this very real struggle for the souls of the elderly have occurred during my visiting experiences.

THE DEVIL'S LIE

Whenever possible, girls from our horse ranch came with me to visit. Most of them were new Christians and eager to share God's love. One afternoon our visit brought us into a room where two ladies resided. The first woman, securely strapped in her wheelchair, had her arms folded on her chest. With her head dropped down, she rocked back and forth, continually emitting unintelligible sounds.

We quickly skirted around her only to discover another "far out" occupant. This tiny, white-haired lady with a quite-prominent nose sat beside her bed in a contraption that looked like an adult high chair on wheels - tray and all. Her gaze concentrated down as she traced her wispy finger back and forth on the tray. With her head cocked sideways so she could see out of her one good eye, she carefully studied her finger's progress.

Since both of these ladies seemed unaware of our presence, we hesitated to try to communicate with either one of them. We looked at each other and shrugged our shoulders as if to say, "Why not?" So we began with the finger tracing lady.

Reading her arm band, we found her name was Sarah. Surprisingly, when we spoke to her, she stopped her methodical tracing. Then, tilting her head sideways, she surveyed us with her big blue eye and smiled. We soon discovered the sweetness of her personality. She was delighted that we had come to see her. We all enjoyed getting to know her, even though she randomly mixed the past and present without realizing it.

We always dropped by Sarah's room whenever we could. Each visit we would gingerly slip past the tied-in lady of strange sounds. Much to our surprise, we observed that Elsie, Sarah's roommate, did have one talent. I say talent because taking off your dress while tied in a wheelchair is no easy task!

On about our fourth visit, I made a suggestion to a rather shy member of our group. "Tracy, will you stand by Elsie and rub her back while we visit Sarah. If you do, maybe it will quiet Elsie and she won't take her dress off while we're here." Tracy reluctantly agreed. Happily, it worked! Elsie left her dress on.

As we walked out the doorway, Tracy ventured somewhat timidly, "I don't think Elsie wanted me to leave!"

"Why would you think that?" I responded.

"I don't know; she just didn't," came the reply.

Suddenly it dawned on me. Of course! There's still a live person in Elsie's confused body. Although she is unable to speak or even to look at us, she is there and has needs - especially to hear of God's love. I turned back toward Elsie, knelt beside her and sang, *For God so Loved the World.* She rocked and emitted garbled sounds, but gave no response to the music. After finishing I whispered to her, "Elsie, God loves you and Jesus loves you too."

She turned, looked me right in the eye and violently hissed, "He does not."

I cringed! But in that instant, God led me to boldly reply, "Oh, yes he does! God loves you and so does Jesus. Satan has lied to you. He thinks he owns you forever, Elsie, but he doesn't; that's why you're still alive. You still have a chance to believe in Jesus today. Don't let Satan lie to you."

I then prayed over her and asked God to give her the understanding to accept Jesus. Shaken, I left the room.

The girls huddled together in the hallway, tears filling their eyes. They knew they had seen Satan's evil work firsthand. We prayed together for Elsie and for ourselves. Two days later, we cautiously returned to pray for Elsie again, but she was gone.

I don't know if she received Jesus that day or not, but I do know she had one more chance. Perhaps, just perhaps, we'll see her in heaven someday.

MENTAL INABILITY

"Senility" is a general term that is used to describe many different kinds of mental impairment. More exactly, the term is "senile dementia". This impairment includes Alzheimer's disease as well as varying degrees of memory loss. These patients should never be treated or spoken to in an infantile way. They deserve patience and respect. When they have difficulty phrasing their thoughts, you may comment, "I have lots of time; don't rush yourself."

Avoid the temptation to finish their sentences when they speak slowly. This interruption will discourage them from verbalizing. Realize that their thought processes may be in top shape but the ability to remember and form words is greatly impaired. Imagine how frustrating that becomes as the days and weeks pass.

Other residents may revert to a helpless, quiet state in which they stay until death takes them. Love them as God does. Remember Jesus said, *"God so loved the world"*. These helpless ones sense and appreciate your attention.[44]

Occasionally, you will be surprised at responses you receive from these quiet ones. As you talk or sing to them, they sometimes join in. For a time, they seem to come back to reality and to the present.

Peoples' reactions to music are quite interesting. Even patients in a terminal condition who are unable to speak will sometimes softly join in singing an old familiar hymn with you. This interesting phenomenon also occurs in patients with "expressive aphasia". Even though they are unable to transfer their thoughts into speech, they can sometimes sing!

As I mentioned, one of my earliest convalescent home surprises was Millie. As my son and I discovered, she would usually only say yes or no, or repeat what you said to her. But she also quoted Bible verses, rapid fire, and sang with us. *"Make a joyful noise unto the Lord"* [45] really applied in her case! Let me assure you that visiting is never dull. Each trip to a home is as varied as the different people living there. It's exciting; you never know what to expect!

LOVE MINISTERS

Sitting day after day without the normal stimulation of the outside world, promotes withdrawal and depression. Your gentle enthusiasm can be so helpful as you take time out of your world to share in theirs. Nurses and staff are paid to be there and they do their jobs. You, however, are there only because you choose to be. This fact alone can touch people who feel abandoned.

So many times they tell me, "Oh, I'm just in here temporarily. I have a home of my own. I'll be going back there soon." Sometimes this is true, but more often it is not. Many times relatives who admit elderly family members to a nursing home tell them this because they feel it will make the transfer easier. Some patients invent this story on their own because they refuse to deal with the reality of their situation. It is really not your concern whether or not they are permanent residents. It is your ministry to reach out and love them.

OPPOSITION FROM
OTHER ROOM OCCUPANTS

Another sobering incident occurred that reminded me of Satan's control over people. I had gone into a room to see Dorcas, one of the most wonderful saints of God I've ever known. Blind and bedridden, she lay on the second bed in the room.

As I entered, I noticed that the other occupant of the room was new. She appeared to be about sixty and in reasonable health, which is unusual for these homes.

I stepped inside, moving toward Dorcas bed. As I passed the first lady, I smiled and nodded.

"Get out of here right now", she snarled.

"I'll try not to disturb you," I carefully replied, "but I've come to see my friend Dorcas today."

"She doesn't want to see you," the woman angrily spouted. "So get out right now."

I replied firmly, "I'm going to see my friend."

As usual, Dorcas was a delight. She and I praised the Lord together and we sang a few songs about Jesus. She was ninety-five years old and probably weighed no more than seventy pounds. She confided in me that day, "The nurses in here work so hard. I try to pray for them as much as I can." Every encounter with Dorcas was a real blessing to me. Upon leaving I prayed, asking God for wisdom to reach the hostile room-mate.

On the way out, I noticed some memorabilia beside the first lady's chair about which I could make a comment. Slowly she thawed and talked with me. As we spoke, I recognized from her name and a picture on her dresser that she was the mother of a reported racketeer. The occupants of this room demonstrated spiritual truth. Satan destroys lives. God builds them.

Dorcas, at ninety-five, was still blessing people and praising God, while the other woman was angry and hated everyone that came into her presence. She (or a demon inside her) had even sought to stop me from seeing Dorcas that day.

Know who you are in Jesus Christ. Believe in the authority that you have. The creator of the universe has told you to go and minister to these helpless ones. God, through the Holy Spirit, will give you the power necessary to defeat the adversary.

Other room occupants may interfere with your visit simply from jealousy and a desire for attention. In this situation, you may elect to cut short your visit and come another time with a friend. Visiting by twos in these rooms is best. Then you can each talk to one person.

CHATTERBOXES

Occasionally, you begin a conversation with someone only to find out that they can speak for ten minutes straight without taking a single breath, or so it seems. It is sad to realize how starved these people are for someone to hear them out.

After awhile, though, you realize their domination of your visiting time is taking away time from others equally needy. You may need to be firm. Simply stand up and excuse yourself. Perhaps say, "You have so much to tell me, but I'm afraid we need another day to finish."

One lady wouldn't let me go even with that. Finally, I just had to interrupt her and say goodbye. As I walked out the door, she was still talking. I felt rude and sad. Maybe the next time I'll interrupt and say, "May I pray for you?" then I'll pray and on the "Amen", exit . . . fast!

Remember, not everyone you'll visit is charming. Some people are selfish and self centered. Don't allow them to take all your time and cause you to neglect the quiet ones.

PAIN AND SUFFERING

Most residents are fairly comfortable physically. Some, however, have pain varying from a common headache to severe pain. God says to,

"Pray one for another, that ye may be healed. The effectual fervent prayer of a righteous man availeth much." [46]

I'm not suggesting that after you pray, the aged body will be twenty-one again, but God does answer prayer. Growing old with grace and being lifted above pain is certainly to be desired.

Perhaps just sitting beside an ailing oldster, holding a feeble hand for awhile, is how the Lord would have you minister.

PROBLEMS WITHIN

You may experience a day of visiting where nothing seems to go well. Could this difficulty be coming from within yourself? If your own heart is not right, you need to turn to the Lord.

The Psalmist says,

> *"If I regard iniquity in my heart the Lord will not hear me."* [47]

Proverbs says,

> *"He that turneth away his ear from hearing the law, even his prayer shall be abomination."* [48]

If some known sin in your life is hindering God's blessing, you need to use God's cleansing system,

> *"If we confess our sins, he is faithful and just to forgive us our sins, and to cleanse us from all un-righteousness."* [49]

God wants to love through you. After you clear up the impediment of sin, He will once again use you to His honor.

Remember to prepare before each visit with prayer and time in God's Word. Physically, the homes may present peace and tranquility, but in reality you are entering a spiritual war zone.

SECTION III

Share/Prepare/Do I Dare?

As shown, visiting in nursing homes is more than saying, "Hi, how are you today?" Hopefully, you now have a variety of ideas on how to minister to the elderly.

This third section presents suggestions for sharing this ministry information with others.

It also contains a chapter of verses listed by topic. Accompanying these verses are comments to help you incorporate scripture into conversation as you minister.

A series of questions about each chapter, finishes the section. Use the questions as a group study guide or for personal review.

Chapter 11

SHARE
(Positive Ways to Spread the Word)

If you feel God has spoken to you through the words in this book, there are seven ways listed in this chapter to spread this information.

VISIT

1. You may decide God is leading you to visit the elderly. If so, go. God will bless you according to his Word.

PRAY

2. Perhaps God wanted you to be familiar with the needs of the elderly and the difficulties that face those who minister to them. Is this added insight calling you to support these needs in prayer?

SHARE

3. Share this book with others; they might become visitors. Some may even trust in Jesus after reading it.

INTRODUCE

4. Introduce this book to directors of local nursing homes. Administrators may wish to distribute them to educate volunteers and to encourage the families of their residents.

GIVE

5. You might know a family with a relative already in a home or about to move into one. You can assist them in their time of difficulty by giving them a copy of this book.

LIBRARY

6. Many churches and Christian groups have lending libraries for their members. Spread the information by presenting several copies to your church. Public libraries also welcome book donations.

INSTRUCT

7. If you have a heart for the elderly and feel the information in this book could benefit them, you can organize an instruction class. Use the book as your textbook and the review questions in chapter 13 as your teaching outline. If the thought of teaching a class is mind-boggling, then enlist the aid of someone with teaching experience.

Try these suggestions for organizing your class:

A. Invite people in your church or group to attend the class by suggesting that everyone either:
   1. Knows someone "inside" a care facility,
   2. Will eventually need to place a dear one in a home, or
   3. Might live there themselves in the future.

B. Tell people you realize that not everyone is called to be a "visitor". Suggest, that after taking this class, they can more effectively pray for the needs of the elderly and those who minister to them.

C. It is important for everyone in the class to have a copy of the book. Much of the encouragement offered is in the form of stories. These cause the reader to sense the emotions connected with volunteerism and with life in a long-term care facility. The rest of the book is more objective information which the class can discuss.

D. The amount of material you can cover depends on the time allotted for your class. You can ask your students to read ahead each week. During class time, the members are led in a group discussion.

E. Challenge the class members to imagine themselves both as visitors and as patients. Try some role playing. Discuss the resulting sensations. Use these results to encourage the students to feel the needs of the elderly.

F. As teacher, be sure to mention and apply the appropriate scriptures from chapter 12.

G. Pray in each class session, for nursing home residents known to class members. Also pray for the Lord to direct class members to their special place of service.

H. Provide a field trip to a local professional home as a part of the class. Your class members need encouragement to apply their newly gained skills.

I. Invite staff members from a local long-term care home to come and speak to your class. Their expertise will provide added insight and will build a good relationship with the home.

Chapter 12

PREPARE
(Spiritual Preparation)

As you visit, you will discover that the seniors you visit feel the same needs that you do. God has answers for each of these needs. You have a message of love and hope to bring to these people. Make certain you are comfortably familiar with God's Word so you can effectively deliver God's message.

The verses in this chapter will recharge your "spiritual batteries". You may decide to study the verses in depth, or perhaps just use the list to review specific topics.

CONTENTS

AVOIDING ARGUMENTS

People crowded together in small living areas develop numerous petty grievances. These minor problems can grow to unrealistic proportions in the confined environment of professional care homes. God's wisdom for handling these interpersonal difficulties will help. There are many ways to avoid the conflicts that occur.

When a man's ways please the Lord, he maketh even his enemies to be at peace with him - Proverbs 16:7.

He that is slow to wrath is of great understanding: but he that is hasty of spirit exalteth folly - Proverbs 14:29.

A soft answer turneth away wrath: but grievous words stir up anger - Proverbs 15:1.

He that covereth a transgression seeketh love; but he that repeateth a matter separateth very friends - Proverbs 17:9.

He that goeth about as a talebearer revealeth secrets: therefore meddle not with him that flattereth with his lips - Proverbs 20:19.

Say not thou, I will recompense evil; but wait on the Lord, and he shall save thee - Proverbs 20:22.

Answer not a fool according to his folly, lest thou also be like unto him - Proverbs 26:4.

And be ye kind one to another, tenderhearted, forgiving one another, even as God for Christ's sake hath forgiven you - Ephesians 4:32.

Only by pride cometh contention: but with the well advised is wisdom -Proverbs 13:10.

Let us not be desirous of vain glory, provoking one another, envying one another - Galatians 5:26.

Judge not, that ye be not judged. - Matthew 7:1, 2.

FAITH

Our best tribute to God's integrity is trusting Him. As a volunteer, the more you trust Him, the more effectively you can minister. In addition, the more scriptures of faith you can share with the residents, the better they can handle this difficult chapter of their lives.

We should never tire of hearing how ordinary people become extraordinary because they placed their faith in God's Word. We can still trust like they did today, if we choose to do so. Read Hebrews 11 - the entire chapter.

The Lord is my strength and my shield; my heart trusted in him, and I am helped: therefore my heart greatly rejoiceth; and with my song will I praise him - Psalm 28:7.

He staggered not at the promise of God through unbelief; but was strong in faith, giving glory to God; And being fully persuaded that, what he had promised, he was able also to perform - Romans 4:20, 21.

Jesus said unto him, If thou canst believe, all things are possible to him that believeth - Mark 9:23.

And he said to the woman, Thy faith hath saved thee; go in peace - Luke 7:50.

Therefore being justified by faith, we have peace with God through our Lord Jesus Christ - Romans 5:1.

Only by faith in God's power, will you be successful. Jesus did not accomplish much when the townspeople would not believe. Believe God will assist you and be true to His Word.

And he did not many mighty works there because of their unbelief - Matthew 13:58.

God asks us to trust Him. As we learn how much He loves us, we stop demanding "why" everything happens as it does. Trust is knowing your loving God has control over life's situations.

For we walk by faith, not by sight. - II Corinthians 5:7.

FEAR AND PEACE

So many times in the Bible, God says, "Fear not" because he knows we are often afraid. All of us, whether volunteers or residents, need to review these verses regularly. We benefit from this continued reassurance just as a child thrives on comfort from a parent. God even promises sweet sleep.

I will both lay me down in peace, and sleep: for thou, Lord, only makest me dwell in safety - Psalm 4:8.

When thou liest down, thou shalt not be afraid: yea, thou shalt lie down, and thy sleep shall be sweet - Proverbs 3:24.

Thou wilt keep him in perfect peace, whose mind is stayed on thee: because he trusteth in thee - Isaiah 26:3.

Fear thou not; for I am with thee: be not dismayed; for I am thy God: I will strengthen thee; yea, I will help thee; yea, I will uphold thee with the right hand of my righteousness. For I the Lord thy God will hold thy right hand, saying unto thee, Fear not; I will help thee - Isaiah 41:10,13.

For God hath not given us the spirit of fear; but of power, and of love, and of a sound mind. - II Timothy 1:7.

*Casting all your care upon him; for he careth for
you - I Peter 5:7.*

FORGIVENESS - WHAT A RELIEF!

Holding on to guilt is destructive. The enemy,
Satan, knows this and will use our past sins as a
weapon against us. Read these verses on forgiveness
and be blessed by the relief you feel. Remember, too,
that some of the older citizens you'll meet still don't
understand the grace of God.

*Blessed is the man unto whom the Lord imputeth
not iniquity, and in whose spirit there is no guile.
I acknowledged my sin unto thee, and mine iniquity have I not hid. I said, I will confess my transgressions unto the Lord; and thou forgavest the
iniquity of my sin. Selah - Psalm 32:2,5.*

*The Lord is merciful and gracious, slow to anger,
and plenteous in mercy. He will not always
chide: neither will he keep his anger for ever. He
hath not dealt with us after our sins; nor
rewarded us according to our iniquities. For as
the heaven is high above the earth, so great is his
mercy toward them that fear him. As far as the
east is from the west, so far hath he removed our
transgressions from us. Like as a father pitieth
his children, so the Lord pitieth them that fear
him. For he knoweth our frame; he remembereth
that we are dust - Psalm 103:8-14.*

Come now, and let us reason together, saith the Lord: though your sins be as scarlet, they shall be as white as snow; though they be red like crimson, they shall be as wool - Isaiah 1:18.

I, even I, am he that blotteth out thy transgressions for mine own sake, and will not remember thy sins - Isaiah 43:25.

If we confess our sins, he is faithful and just to forgive us our sins, and to cleanse us from all unrighteousness - I John 1:9.

LIFE IS SHORT

Looking at the whole scope of existence, life on earth is immeasurably short compared to eternity. As we become convinced of this, we are motivated to apply whatever time we have to eternal values.

We need also to carry this truth to our older friends as a warning and as a comfort.

Lord, make me to know mine end, and the measure of my days, what it is; that I may know how frail I am. Behold, thou hast made my days as an handbreadth; and mine age is as nothing before thee: verily every man at his best state is altogether vanity. Selah - Psalm 39:4, 5.

So teach us to number our days, that we may apply our hearts unto wisdom - Psalm 90:12.

O that they were wise, that they understood this, that they would consider their latter end! - Deuteronomy 32:29.

For here have we no continuing city, but we seek one to come - Hebrews 13:14.

Whereas ye know not what shall be on the morrow. For what is your life? It is even a vapour, that appeareth for a little time, and then vanisheth away - James 4:14.

See then that ye walk circumspectly, not as fools, but as wise. Redeeming the time, because the days are evil - Ephesians 5:15, 16.

LONG LIFE

God designed the seasons of life. The Bible teaches us that long life is a blessing from God. You'll meet many people in nursing homes that have applied these truths. When you do, you'll walk out with a firmer spiritual step.

But the path of the just is as the shining light, that shineth more and more unto the perfect day - Proverbs 4:18.

For by me thy days shall be multiplied, and the years of thy life shall be increased - Proverbs 9:11.

The fear of the Lord tendeth to life: and he that hath it shall abide satisfied; he shall not be visited with evil - Proverbs 19:23.

The glory of young men is their strength: and the beauty of old men is the grey head - Proverbs 20:29.

Thou shalt rise up before the hoary head, and honor the face of the old man, and fear thy God: I am the Lord - Leviticus 19:32.

My son, forget not my law; but let thine heart keep my commandments. For length of days, and long life, and peace, shall they add to thee - Proverbs 3:1-2.

O God, thou hast taught me from my youth: and hitherto have I declared thy wondrous works. Now also when I am old and greyheaded, O God, forsake me not; until I have shewed thy strength unto this generation, and thy power to every one that is to come - Psalm 71:17, 18.

LOVE IS A COMMAND

God's love for us, and our love toward the elderly needs to be verbalized many times as we minister. Love is not a nebulous feeling over which we have no control. We are commanded to love.

Review these scriptures often:

And thou shalt love the Lord thy God with all thy heart, and with all thy soul, and with all thy mind, and with all thy strength: this is the first commandment. And the second is like, namely this, Thou shalt love thy neighbour as thyself. There is none other commandment greater than these - Mark 12: 30, 31.

A new commandment I give unto you, That ye love one another; as I have loved you, that ye also love one another. By this shall all men know that ye are my disciples, if ye have love one to another - John 13:34-35.

Let love be without dissimulation. Abhor that which is evil; cleave to that which is good. Be kindly affectioned one to another with brotherly love; in honour preferring one another - Romans 12:9, 10.

Be ye therefore followers of God, as dear children; And walk in love, as Christ also hath loved us, and hath given himself for us an offering and a sacrifice to God for a sweetsmelling savour - Ephesians 5:1-2.

Beloved, let us love one another: for love is of God; and every one that loveth is born of God, and knoweth God. He that loveth not knoweth not God; for God is love. In this was manifested the love of God toward us, because that God sent

his only begotten Son into the world, that we
might live through him. Herein is love, not that
we loved God, but that he loved us, and sent his
Son to be the propitiation for our sins. Beloved,
if God so loved us, we ought also to love one
another. We love him, because he first loved us.
If a man say, I love God, and hateth his brother,
he is a liar: for he that loveth not his brother
whom he hath seen, how can he love God whom
he hath not seen? And this commandment have
we from him, That he who loveth God love his
brother also - I John 4:7-11, 19-21.

MUCH ABOUT HEAVEN

The excitement of a good trip begins during the
planning stages. We all love reading the travel
brochure that describes our destination in inviting
terms. So it is with aging Christians whose bodies are
failing; they would like to talk about the trip they're
about to take. The scriptures describing heaven will be
uplifting both to you and to the people with whom you
share. Read Revelation chapters 21 and 22.

There's a day coming when we will move to our permanent home prepared for us by Jesus. It's a custom
home, designed for us with love. This brings present
peace to our hearts, as we look at promises for the future.

Let not your heart be troubled: ye believe in God,
believe also in me. In my Father's house are
many mansions: if it were not so, I would have

told you. I go to prepare a place for you. And if I go and prepare a place for you, I will come again, and receive you unto myself; that where I am, there ye may be also - John 14:1-3.

And he shewed me a pure river of water of life, clear as crystal, proceeding out of the throne of God and of the Lamb. In the midst of the street of it, and on either side of the river, was there the tree of life, which bare twelve manner of fruits, and yielded her fruit every month: and the leaves of the tree were for the healing of the nations. And there shall be no more curse: but the throne of God and of the Lamb shall be in it; and his servants shall serve him: And they shall see his face; and his name shall be in their foreheads. And there shall be no night there; and they need no candle, neither light of the sun; for the Lord God giveth them light: and they shall reign for ever and ever - Revelation 22:1-5.

PRAISE GOD!

When we have bodily discomfort or perceived lack of value, we find it hard to praise God. Interestingly, as we obey God by praising him even when circumstances appear bleak, we begin to experience his love and sustaining strength. This truth must be shared.

Praise is infectious. The more naturally praise comes out of your mouth, the more likely people around you will begin to praise God. The Lord is honored as we submit to his supreme wisdom with a smile.

Why art thou cast down, O my soul? and why art thou disquieted within me? hope thou in God: for I shall yet praise him, who is the health of my countenance, and my God - Psalm 42:11.

Give thanks unto the Lord, call upon his name, make known his deeds among the people. Sing unto him, sing psalms unto him, talk ye of all his wondrous works. Give unto the Lord, the glory due unto his name: bring an offering, and come before him: worship the Lord in the beauty of holiness. O give thanks unto the Lord; for he is good; for his mercy endureth for ever - I Chronicles 16:8, 9, 29, 34.

Let the redeemed of the Lord say so, whom he hath redeemed from the hand of the enemy; Oh that men would praise the Lord for his goodness, and for his wonderful works to the children of men! - Psalm 107:2, 8.

Bless the Lord, O my soul: and all that is within me, bless his holy name. Bless the Lord, O my soul, and forget not all his benefits - Psalm 103:1, 2.

I will sing of the mercies of the Lord for ever: with my mouth will I make known thy faithfulness to all generations - Psalm 89:1.

Because thy lovingkindness is better than life, my lips shall praise thee. Thus will I bless thee while I live: I will lift up my hands in thy name. My soul shall be satisfied as with marrow and fatness; and my mouth shall praise thee with joyful lips: When I remember thee upon my bed, and meditate on thee in the night watches. Because thou hast been my help, therefore in the shadow of thy wings will I rejoice - Psalm 63:3-7.

This is the day which the Lord hath made; we will rejoice and be glad in it - Psalm 118:24.

Speaking to yourselves in psalms and hymns and spiritual songs, singing and making melody in your heart to the Lord; Giving thanks always for all things unto God and the Father in the name of our Lord Jesus Christ - Ephesians 5:19, 20.

God tells us to live, think and speak about that which is positive. In doing this we are obeying God and also lifting others from the negative pull of the world.

Finally, brethren, whatsoever things are true, whatsoever things are honest, whatsoever things are just, whatsoever things are pure, whatsoever things are lovely, whatsoever things are of good report; if there be any virtue, and if there be any praise, think on these things - Philippians 4:8.

PRAYER

Prayer is communication with God. As Christians, we have the privilege of receiving help from the creator of the universe. What a privilege! Pray for your elderly friends - these dear creations of God. Pray, not just in your devotions at home, but also as you visit. Listen to the Holy Spirit's promptings. As you pray, it is particularly meaningful to the residents if you touch their hand or shoulder.

Discuss prayer with them. Some people are hesitant to "bother" God with their needs. Show them from the scriptures how interested God is in the smallest details of their lives.

The young lions do lack, and suffer hunger: but they that seek the Lord shall not want any good thing. The eyes of the Lord are upon the righteous, and his ears are open unto their cry - Psalm 34:10,15.

The Lord upholdeth all that fall, and raiseth up all those that be bowed down. The eyes of all wait upon thee; and thou givest them their meat in due season. Thou openest thine hand, and satisfiest the desire of every living thing. The Lord is righteous in all his ways, and holy in all his works. The Lord is nigh unto all them that call upon him, to all that call upon him in truth. He will fulfill the desire of them that fear him: he also will hear their cry, and will save them - Psalm 145:14-19.

And all things, whatsoever ye shall ask in prayer, believing, ye shall receive - Matthew 21:22.

Therefore I say unto you, What things soever ye desire, when ye pray, believe that ye receive them, and ye shall have them - Mark 11:24.

If ye abide in me, and my words abide in you, ye shall ask what ye will, and it shall be done unto you - John 15:7.

For we have not an high priest which cannot be touched with the feeling of our infirmities; but was in all points tempted like as we are, yet without sin. Let us therefore come boldly unto the throne of grace, that we may obtain mercy, and find grace to help in time of need - Hebrews 4:15, 16.

And whatsoever we ask, we receive of him, because we keep his commandments, and do those things that are pleasing in his sight - I John 3:22.

And this is the confidence that we have in him, that, if we ask any thing according to his will, he heareth us: And if we know that he hear us, whatsoever we ask, we know that we have the petitions that we desired of him - I John 5:14, 15.

God has a design for healing and encouragement. His design may involve your praying for people's needs.

Is any sick among you? let him call for the elders of the church, and let them pray over him, anointing him with oil in the name of the Lord: And the prayer of faith shall save the sick, and the Lord shall raise him up; and if he have committed sins, they shall be forgiven him. Confess your faults one to another, and pray one for another that ye may be healed. The effectual fervent prayer of a righteous man availeth much - James 5:14-16.

There are times when God will not listen to our prayers. The Bible says this blockage is because of disobedience.

The sacrifice of the wicked is an abomination to the Lord: but the prayer of the upright is his delight - Proverbs 15:8.

He that turneth away his ear from hearing the law, even his prayer shall be abomination - Proverbs 28:9.

RELIGION - IS IT GOOD?

Religion, as described in the Bible, is man's attempt to reach God. It is critical that you, as a spiritual ambassador of God, learn to perceive the difference between trusting in a man-made organization and having a saving faith in Jesus Christ. Read the scriptures listed under "religion". Practice viewing life as God does. Then, with the discernment of the Holy Spirit, you will discover people who are trusting in a church affiliation rather than in God's personal provision for them.

For I bear them record that they have a zeal of God, but not according to knowledge. For they being ignorant of God's righteousness, and going about to establish their own righteousness, have not submitted themselves unto the righteousness of God - Romans 10:2, 3.

For thou desirest not sacrifice; else I would give it: thou delightest not in burnt-offering. The sacrifices of God are a broken spirit: a broken and contrite heart, O God, thou wilt not despise - Psalm 51:16, 17.

Just because a church uses the name of Jesus Christ does not mean it teaches God's Holy Word, the Bible. Many have departed from the truth of God and invented their own system.

For the pastors are become brutish, and have not sought the Lord: therefore they shall not prosper, and all their flocks shall be scattered - Jeremiah 10:21.

Beware of false prophets, which come to you in sheep's clothing, but inwardly they are ravening wolves. Not every one that saith unto me, Lord, Lord, shall enter into the kingdom of heaven; but he that doeth the will of my Father which is in heaven. Many will say to me in that day, Lord, Lord, have we not prophesied in thy name? and

*in thy name have cast out devils? and in thy name
done many wonderful works? And then will I
profess unto them, I never knew you: depart from
me, ye that work iniquity - Matthew 7:15, 21-23.*

*Woe   unto   you,   scribes   and   Pharisees,
hypocrites! for ye are like unto whited sepul-
chres, which indeed appear beautiful outward,
but are within full of dead men's bones, and of
all uncleanness. Even so ye also outwardly appear righteous unto men, but within ye are full
of hypocrisy and iniquity - Matthew 23:27, 28.*

To claim the name of God is not enough. Being
aware of the existence of God and Jesus is admirable
but incomplete. It is also good to learn that Jesus died
on the cross and rose from the dead. However, to
receive any personal application in our lives, we must
place our faith in Jesus as our only way to heaven.

*For unto us was the gospel preached, as well as
unto them; but the word preached did not profit
them, not being mixed with faith in them that
heard it - Hebrews 4:2.*

Being a good person, doing your best not to hurt
others is not enough to make us pure, ready to stand in
the presence of God - that is why Jesus had to die to
pay the penalty for our sin and thus make cleansing
available to us.

*I do not frustrate the grace of God: for if
righteousness come by the law, then Christ is
dead in vain - Galatians 2:21.*

Stand fast therefore in the liberty wherewith Christ hath made us free, and be not entangled again with the yoke of bondage. Christ is become of no effect unto you, whosoever of you are justified by the law; ye are fallen from grace - Galatians 5:1,4.

Having a form of godliness, but denying the power thereof: from such turn away. Ever learning, and never able to come to the knowledge of the truth - II Timothy 3:5,7.

RESISTING SATAN

The scriptures in this section help volunteers say with firmness, along with the Apostle Paul, *"Lest Satan should get an advantage of us: for we are not ignorant of his devices."* - I Corinthians 2:11. Be sure to read Ephesians 6:10-17.

Then saith Jesus unto him, Get thee hence, Satan: for it is written, Thou shalt worship the Lord thy God, and him only shalt thou serve - Matthew 4:10.

There is a real individual named Satan who actively attempts to stop people from receiving Christ. If he does lose anyone to God, he has an alternative plan. He knows how to discourage, bring fear and pull a new believer into sin.

Submit yourselves therefore to God. Resist the devil, and he will flee from you - James 4:7.

Be sober, be vigilant; because your adversary the devil, as a roaring lion, walketh about, seeking whom he may devour - I Peter 5:8.

For such are false apostles, deceitful workers, transforming themselves into the apostles of Christ. And no marvel; for Satan himself is transformed into an angel of light. Therefore it is no great thing if his ministers also be transformed as the ministers of righteousness; whose end shall be according to their works - II Corinthians 11:13-15.

Ye are of God, little children, and have overcome them: because greater is he that is in you, than he that is in the world - I John 4:4.

REWARDS

How exciting to be able to discuss heavenly rewards with believers, who are about ready to step into heaven itself! It's also an uplifting experience to review all the blessings these seniors have already received during a lifetime of walking with the Lord. Many bubble over with appreciation for all that God has done for them. Encouraged others to recount their blessings.

Also, on those down days when you don't feel like reaching out to these forgotten ones, review these verses. You, too, will be blessed. God's promise of rewards for a life of service apply to you right now.

Cast not away therefore your confidence, which hath great recompense of reward. For ye have need of patience, that, after ye have done the will of God, ye might receive the promise - Hebrews 10:35,36.

The thief cometh not, but for to steal, and to kill, and to destroy: I am come that they might have life, and that they might have it more abundantly. I am the good shepherd: the good shepherd giveth his life for the sheep - John 10:10,11.

How exciting to realize that God has future interesting plans for us in heaven. Rewards and crowns are promised.

I have fought a good fight. I have finished my course, I have kept the faith: Henceforth there is laid up for me a crown of righteousness, which the Lord, the righteous judge, shall give me at that day: and not to me only, but unto all them also that love his appearing - II Timothy 4:7,8.

For other foundation can no man lay than that is laid, which is Jesus Christ. Now if any man build upon this foundation gold, silver, precious stones, wood, hay stubble; Every man's work shall be made manifest: for the day shall declare it, because it shall be revealed by fire; and the fire shall try every man's work of what sort it is. If any man's work abide which he hath built thereupon, he shall receive a reward. If any

man's work shall be burned, he shall suffer loss:
but he himself shall be saved; yet so as by fire - I
Corinthians 3:11-15.

SALVATION

Be sure to review the verses in this section as God
says,

To be ready always to give an answer to every
man that asketh you a reason of the hope that is
in you - I Peter 3:15.

As you explain salvation, pray for the Holy Spirit to
guide you to use the right scriptures and words. It's
very important to read John 3:1-36. The person to
whom you're presenting salvation needs to understand:

- All people are in a lost condition and destined
  for Hell because of their sin;

- Jesus, as God and man, lived a sinless life and
  willingly went to the cross;

- Jesus was punished for us as he died on the
  cross;

- Jesus conquered death by his resurrection and
  continues to represent us in heaven;

- and, to receive this gift of forgiveness, we must
  tell God we believe the record about His son
  and desire the salvation that He offers.

The law of the Lord is perfect, converting the
soul: the testimony of the Lord is sure, making
wise the simple. The statutes of the Lord are

right, rejoicing the heart: the commandment of the Lord is pure, enlightening the eyes. - Psalm 19:7, 8.

O taste and see that the Lord is good: blessed is the man that trusteth in him - Psalm 34:8.

The fear of the Lord is the beginning of knowledge: but fools despise wisdom and instruction - Proverbs 1:7.

Not everyone places their trust in Jesus Christ. In fact, a large segment of mankind ignores God's plan.

Enter ye in at the strait gate: for wide is the gate, and broad is the way, that leadeth to destruction, and many there be which go in thereat: Because strait is the gate, and narrow is the way, which leadeth unto life, and few there be that find it - Matthew 7:13, 14.

Come to Jesus. Give your cares and worries to him.

Come unto me, all ye that labour and are heavy laden, and I will give you rest. Take my yoke upon you, and learn of me; for I am meek and lowly in heart: and ye shall find rest unto your souls. For my yoke is easy, and my burden is light - Matthew 11:28-30.

There is no work we can do to add to or earn salvation. Jesus did it all and we appropriate it only by faith. Ask and receive. Jesus promised paradise to the thief hanging next to Him on the cross. The thief had nothing to offer. He joined no church, did no good works, and could obey no ordinances. He simply believed in Jesus.

And he said unto Jesus, Lord, remember me when thou comest into thy kingdom. And Jesus said unto him, Verily I say unto thee, Today shalt thou be with me in paradise - Luke 23:42, 43.

No man is justified by the law in the sight of God, it is evident: for, The just shall live by faith - Galatians 3:11.

Becoming a child of God is a supernatural experience. It's obtained only by faith in God's provision of Jesus Christ as Savior.

But as many as received him, to them gave he power to become the sons of God, even to them that believe on his name: Which were born, not of blood, nor of the will of the flesh, nor of the will of man, but of God - John 1:12, 13.

Verily, verily, I say unto you, He that heareth my word, and believeth on him that sent me, hath everlasting life, and shall not come into condemnation; but is passed from death unto life - John 5:24.

Then said they unto him, What shall we do, that we might work the works of God? Jesus answered and said unto them, This is the work of God, that ye believe on him whom he hath sent. And Jesus said unto them, I am the bread of life:

he that cometh to me shall never hunger; and he that believeth on me shall never thirst. And this is the will of him that sent me, that every one which seeth the Son, and believeth on him, may have everlasting life: and I will raise him up at the last day. Verily, verily, I say unto you, He that believeth on me hath everlasting life - John 6:28, 29, 35, 40, 47.

But these are written, that ye might believe that Jesus is the Christ, the Son of God; and that believing ye might have life through his name - John 20:31.

Neither is there salvation in any other: for there is none other name under heaven given among men, whereby we must be saved - Acts 4:12.

And they said, Believe on the Lord Jesus Christ, and thou shalt be saved, and thy house - Acts 16:31.

For therein is the righteousness of God revealed from faith to faith: as it is written, The just shall live by faith - Romans 1:17.

Being justified freely by his grace through the redemption that is in Christ Jesus: Therefore we conclude that a man is justified by faith without the deeds of the law - Romans 3:24, 28.

That if thou shalt confess with thy mouth the Lord Jesus, and shalt believe in thine heart that God hath raised him from the dead, thou shalt be saved. For with the heart man believeth unto righteousness; and with the mouth confession is made unto salvation - Romans 10:9, 10.

For there is one God, and one mediator between God and man, the man Christ Jesus - I Timothy 2:5.

There is no work you can do to earn salvation. You can only receive it as a free gift from God.

For if Abraham were justified by works, he hath whereof to glory; but not before God. For what saith the scripture? Abraham believed God, and it was counted unto him for righteousness. Now to him that worketh is the reward not reckoned of grace, but of debt. But to him that worketh not, but believeth on him that justifieth the ungodly, his faith is counted for righteousnes. - Romans 4:2-5.

For the wages of sin is death; but the gift of God is eternal life through Jesus Christ our Lord - Romans 6:23.

And you hath he quickened, who were dead in trespasses and sins: For by grace are ye saved through faith; and that not of yourselves: it is the gift of God: Not of works, lest any man should boast - Ephesians 2:1,8,9.

Not by works of righteousness which we have done, but according to his mercy he saved us, by the washing of regeneration, and renewing of the Holy Ghost - Titus 3:5.

These things have I written unto you that believe on the name of the Son of God; that ye may know that ye have eternal life, and that ye may believe on the name of the Son of God - I John 5:13.

Make sure the measuring stick for your life is the Lord, not other people.

For we dare not make ourselves of the number, or compare ourselves with some that commend themselves: but they measuring themselves by themselves, and comparing themselves among themselves, are not wise. For not he that commendeth himself is approved, but whom the Lord commendeth - II Corinthians 10:12,18.

SELF-WORTH

Because of the warehouse effect of professional care homes, it becomes difficult for residents to believe that anyone loves them. Many of the staff members I've encountered make efforts to counteract this feeling of worthlessness, but help from the outside is sorely needed.

As you prepare for visiting by reading the verses in this section, you too will feel more loved. The "self-worth" that God has to offer, surpasses all material and psychological encouragement.

> *Are not two sparrows sold for a farthing? and one of them shall not fall on the ground without your Father. But the very hairs of your head are all numbered. Fear ye not therefore, ye are of more value than many sparrows - Matthew 10:29-31.*

You are uniquely designed by God.

> *For we are his workmanship, created in Christ Jesus unto good works, which God hath before ordained that we should walk in them - Ephesians 2:10.*

God put a crown on your head when you trusted in Jesus. The King of the universe transformed you into royalty. He is with you everywhere - all the time. Such a blessing! Don't miss a word of Psalm 139:1-18 and Matthew 6: 33-35.

SIN - DOES IT EXIST?

The average person's definition of sin covers only the most heinous and deliberate of wrongdoings. God views sin from a different perspective. Everyone will face God one day. He will examine how each person settled the sin problem in his life. These verses show that denial of sin in our lives is not a new evasion.

> *God looked down from heaven upon the children of men, to see if there were any*

that did understand, that did seek God. Every one of them is gone back: they are altogether become filthy; there is none that doeth good, no, not one - Psalm 53:2, 3.

The heart is deceitful above all things, and desperately wicked: who can know it? - Jeremiah 17:9.

Can any hide himself in secret places that I shall not see him? saith the Lord. Do not I fill heaven and earth? saith the Lord - Jeremiah 23:24.

As it is written, There is none righteous, no, not one: Therefore by the deeds of the law there shall no flesh be justified in his sight: for by the law is the knowledge of sin. For all have sinned, and come short of the glory of God - Romans 3:10, 20, 23.

Our sins condemn us, but praise God, He provided a way to escape!

For he hath made him to be sin for us, who knew no sin; that we might be made the righteousness of God in him - II Corinthians 5:21.

For scarcely for a righteous man will one die: yet peradventure for a good man some would even dare to die. But God commendeth his love toward us, in that, while we were yet sinners, Christ died for us - Romans 5:7,8.

If you harbor sin and don't confess it to God, He will not hear your prayers. You can't expect to prosper in this condition. For the eyes of the Lord are over the righteous, and his ears are open unto their prayers: but the face of the Lord is against them that do evil - I Peter 3:12.

If I regard iniquity in my heart, the Lord will not hear me - Psalm 66:18.

He that covereth his sins shall not prosper: but whoso confesseth and forsaketh them shall have mercy - Proverbs 28:13.

Behold, the Lord's hand is not shortened, that it cannot save; neither his ear heavy, that it cannot hear: But your iniquities have separated between you and your God, and your sins have hid his face from you, that he will not hear - Isaiah 59:1, 2.

God even considers rebellion, stubbornness and not obeying Him, as evil as witchcraft and idol worship.

And Samuel said, Hath the Lord as great delight in burnt-offerings and sacrifices, as in obeying the voice of the Lord? Behold, to obey is better than sacrifice, and to hearken than the fat of rams. For rebellion is as the sin of witchcraft, and stubbornness is as iniquity and idolatry. Because thou has rejected the word of the Lord, he

*hath also rejected thee from being king- I Samuel
15:22-23.*

When you involve yourself in sin, don't try to find
someone who will tell you it's all right to continue.
God says that adds to your sin.

*Woe to the rebellious children, saith the Lord,
that take counsel, but not of me; and that cover
with a covering, but not of my spirit, that they
may add to sin - Isaiah 30:1.*

God will never allow any pressure or test that is too
much for you. He will always provide a way out. Look
for it.

*Wherefore let him that thinketh he standeth take
heed lest he fall. There hath no temptation taken
you but such as is common to man: but God is
faithful, who will not suffer you to be tempted
above that ye are able; but will with the temptation also make a way to escape, that ye may be
able to bear it - I Corinthians 10:13,23.*

SO MANY PROMISES

How many promises from the Bible have you discovered? How many could you share with another person? There are more than 6,000! How wonderful it is
to read the Bible and discover the many ways God can
provide for us.   You will receive blessings by reading
(and believing) these verses of promise. Familiarize
yourself with them in order to share hope with all those
you meet.

God is our refuge and strength, a very present help in trouble - Psalm 46:1.

For the Lord God is a sun and shield: the Lord will give grace and glory: no good thing will he withhold from them that walk uprightly - Psalm 84:11.

The 23rd Psalm has familiar words of comfort. They only have meaning to us ,though, when we can say *"The Lord Jesus is MY shepherd."* Review the 23rd Psalm. Give God time to work out situations. He will come through.

Wait on the Lord: be of good courage, and he shall strengthen thine heart: wait, I say, on the Lord - Psalm 27:14.

Every word of God is pure: he is a shield unto them that put their trust in him - Proverbs 30:5.

Now thanks be unto God, which always causeth us to triumph in Christ, and maketh manifest the savour of his knowledge by us in every place - II Corinthians 2:14.

Yes, He sees you and knows your need. God offers you peace beyond anything the world can offer. Be brave. The Creator of the universe is leading the way for you. No situation is too hard for God.

A father of the fatherless, and a judge of the widows, is God in his holy habitation. God set-teth the solitary in families: he bringeth out those which are bound with chains: but the rebellious dwell in a dry land - Psalm 68:5, 6.

For he shall deliver the needy when he crieth, the poor also, and him that hath no helper - Psalm 72:12.

Great peace have they which love thy law: and nothing shall offend them - Psalm 119:165.

Be strong and of good courage, fear not, nor be afraid of them: for the Lord thy God, he it is that doth go with thee; he will not fail thee, nor forsake thee. And the Lord, he it is that doth go before thee; he will be with thee, he will not fail thee, neither forsake thee: fear not, neither be dismayed - Deuteronomy 31:6, 8.

I can do all things through Christ which strengtheneth me - Philippians 4:13.

God promises long life and peace as a reward for being obedient to His Word during your life.

With long life will I satisfy him, and shew him my salvation - Psalm 91:16.

God has uplifting and challenging words for us in the next familiar verses. These words provide even deeper meaning when we consider the preceding chapter. Jesus had just turned down all the tempting offers that Satan could conjure up to entice him then shows by contrast what God has to offer us. Read Matthew 5:3-12.

SUFFERING - A REALITY!

Suffering - do we bring it on ourselves? Is it from God to refine us? Is it from Satan and faith in God would remove it? You will see pain and suffering as you visit the elderly. If you hope to meet their real needs as you visit, I suggest you thoroughly study the Bible on this subject. Your feelings about suffering affect your ministry as a volunteer.

If we base our beliefs solely on what we hear from others, our theology is weak. We must read for ourselves and inquire of the Holy Spirit Who is the only infallible teacher.

Sometimes suffering results from unwise or ungodly behavior. If this is the case, we need to submit to God's loving discipline and return to a life of faith and obedience. Other times, through no fault of our own, we feel the weight of the sinful world in which we live. God will take that load and carry it for you. There is a way. He feels your pain and cares.

For his anger endureth but a moment; in his favour is life: weeping may endure for a night, but joy cometh in the morning - Psalm 30:5.

Many are the afflictions of the righteous: but the Lord delivereth him out of them all - Psalm 34:19.

Cast thy burden upon the Lord, and he shall sustain thee: he shall never suffer the righteous to be moved - Psalm 55:22.

Unless thy law had been my delight, I should then have perished in mine affliction - Psalm 119:92.

I will lift up mine eyes unto the hills, from whence cometh my help. My help cometh from the Lord, which made heaven and earth - Psalm 121:1, 2.

They that sow in tears shall reap in joy - Psalm 126:5.

I cried unto the Lord with my voice; with my voice unto the Lord did I make my supplication. I poured out my complaint before him; I shewed before him my trouble. When my spirit was over-whelmed within me, then thou knewest my path. In the way wherein I walked have they privily laid a snare for me. I looked on my right hand, and beheld, but there was no man that would know me: refuge failed me; no man cared for my soul. I cried unto thee, O Lord: I said, Thou art my refuge and my portion in the land of the living. Attend unto my cry; for I am brought very low: deliver me from my persecutors; for they are stronger than I. Bring my soul out of prison, that I may praise thy name: the righteous shall com-pass me about; for thou shalt deal bountifully with me - Psalm 142:1-7.

Blessed be God, even the Father of our Lord Jesus Christ, the Father of mercies, and the God of all comfort; Who comforteth us in all our tribulation, that we may be able to comfort them which are in any trouble, by the comfort wherewith we ourselves are comforted of God - II Corinthians 1:3, 4.

For what glory is it, if, when ye be buffeted for your faults, ye shall take it patiently? but if, when ye do well, and suffer for it, ye take it patiently, this is acceptable with God - I Peter 2:20.

And ye have forgotten the exhortation which speaketh unto you as unto children, My son, despise not thou the chastening of the Lord, nor faint when thou art rebuked of him: For whom the Lord loveth he chasteneth, and scourgeth every son whom he receiveth. If ye endure chastening, God dealeth with you as with sons; for what son is he whom the father chasteneth not? Now no chastening for the present seemeth to be joyous, but grievous: nevertheless afterward it yieldeth the peaceable fruit of righteousness unto them which are exercised thereby - Hebrews 12:5-7, 11.

TEMPORARY BODIES

Most of us on planet Earth have spent more time providing for our physical needs than in pursuing spiritual growth. As a consequence, when our body grows old and declines in ability, we find confusion and fear begin to dominate our thoughts. At this time, scriptures which show that our bodies are only a house in which the "real" person lives, become a real comfort.

What? Know ye not that your body is the temple of the Holy Ghost which is in you, which ye have of God, and ye are not your own? For ye are bought with a price: therefore glorify God in your body, and in your spirit, which are God's - I Corinthians 6:19, 20.

Know ye not that ye are the temple of God, and that the Spirit of God dwelleth in you?- I Corinthians 3:16.

For I reckon that the sufferings of this present time are not worthy to be compared with the glory which shall be revealed in us - Romans 8:18.

For which cause we faint not; but though our outward man perish, yet the inward man is renewed day by day. For our light affliction, which is but for a moment, worketh for us a far more exceeding and eternal weight of glory; While we look not at the things which are seen, but at the things which are not seen: for the things which are seen are temporal; but the things which are not seen are eternal - II Corinthians 4:16-18.

Some day, as believers, we will have a new body similar to the one Jesus received after resurrection.

Behold, what manner of love the Father hath bestowed upon us, that we should be called the sons of God: therefore the world knoweth us not, because it knew him not. Beloved, now are we the sons of God, and it doth not yet appear what we shall be: but we know that, when he shall appear, we shall be like him; for we shall see him as he is - I John 3:1, 2.

Who shall change our vile body, that it may be fashioned like unto his glorious body, according to the working whereby he is able even to subdue all things to himself- Philippians 3:21

WE ALL NEED ASSURANCE

All of us need the assurance of God's love and keeping power. Those in the twilight years of life, however, are particularly in need of this encouragement. Your personal confidence and knowledge of God's promises in this area are greatly appreciated by those you encounter.

This message of love and security could also draw some of the elderly into first-time faith in Jesus.

And we know that all things work together for good to them that love God, to them who are the called according to his purpose. For whom he did foreknow, he also did predestinate to be conformed to the image of his Son, that he might be the firstborn among many brethren. Moreover whom he did predestinate, them he also called: and whom he called, them he also justified: and whom he justified, them he also glorified. What shall we then say to these things? If God be for us, who can be against us? He that spared not his own Son, but delivered him up for us all, how shall he not with him also freely give us all things? Who shall lay anything to the charge of God's elect? It is God that justifieth. Who is he that condemneth? It is Christ that died, yea rather, that is risen again, who is even at the right hand of God, who also maketh intercession for us. Who shall separate us from the love of Christ? Shall tribulation, or distress, or persecution, or famine, or nakedness, or peril, or sword? As it is written, For thy sake we are killed all the day long; we are accounted as sheep for the slaughter. Nay, in all these things we are more than conquerors through him that loved us. For I am persuaded, that neither death, nor life, nor angels, nor principalities, nor powers, nor things present, nor things to come, Nor height, nor depth, nor any other creature, shall be able to separate us from the love of God, which is in Christ Jesus our Lord - Romans 8:28-39.

God is not in the business of rejecting those who seek Him nor does he throw out those who have come. He is quite capable. God will not lose you. He also wants you to be confident and comfortable when coming to him for help. The peace He offers is beyond anything the world system has to offer.

All that the Father giveth me shall come to me; and him that cometh to me I will in no wise cast out - John 6:37.

In the fear of the Lord is strong confidence: and his children shall have a place of refuge - Proverbs 14:26.

He that hath my commandments, and keepeth them, he it is that loveth me: and he that loveth me shall be loved of my Father, and I will love him, and will manifest myself to him. Peace I leave with you, my peace I give unto you: not as the world giveth, give I unto you. Let not your heart be troubled, neither let it be afraid - John 14:21, 27.

My sheep hear my voice, and I know them, and they follow me: And I give unto them eternal life; and they shall never perish, neither shall any man pluck them out of my hand. My Father, which gave them me, is greater than all; and no man is able to pluck them out of my Father's hand - John 10:27-29.

Being confident of this very thing, that he which hath begun a good work in you will perform it until the day of Jesus Christ - Philippians 1:6.

He that hath the Son hath life; and he that hath not the Son of God hath not life. These things have I written unto you that believe on the name of the Son of God; that ye may know that ye have eternal life, and that ye may believe on the name of the Son of God - I John 5:12, 13.

Jesus said unto her, I am the resurrection, and the life: he that believeth in me, though he were dead, yet shall he live: And whosoever liveth and believeth in me shall never die. Believest thou this? - John 11:25, 26.

If you've been born again by faith in Jesus Christ you are God's property; honor him. The Holy Spirit in our life is the guarantee or stamp of ownership that marks us as "property of God".

In whom ye also trusted, after that ye heard the word of truth, the gospel of your salvation: in whom also after that ye believed, ye were sealed with that holy Spirit of promise, Which is the earnest of our inheritance until the redemption of the purchased possession, unto the praise of his glory - Ephesians 1:13, 14.

And grieve not the holy Spirit of God, whereby ye are sealed unto the day of redemption - Ephesians 4:30.

God does deal with the sins of His children as any loving father would. However, He always honors His relationship with them.

Yes, we all still sin but God has provided a way for forgiveness. Confess each sin to him. He'll forgive those sins and the others you aren't yet mature enough to recognize.

If his children forsake my law, and walk not in my judgments; If they break my statutes, and keep not my commandments; Then will I visit their transgression with the rod, and their iniquity with stripes. Nevertheless my lovingkindness will I not utterly take from him, nor suffer my faithfulness to fail. My covenant will I not break, nor alter the thing that is gone out of my lips - Psalm 89:30-34.

If we say that we have no sin, we deceive ourselves, and the truth is not in us. If we confess our sins, he is faithful and just to forgive us our sins, and to cleanse us from all unrighteousness. If we say that we have not sinned, we make him a liar, and his word is not in us - I John 1:8-10.

WHAT ABOUT DEATH

What can you say to an aged person who will soon die?   The Bible explains that we are born to die, but Jesus died so that we could live. Jesus conquered the curse of death and promises to be with us, even during the dying process. We need to make sure those we comfort have an accurate understanding of how to trust in Jesus as their Savior.

Try reading these verses to become more comfortable with the dying experience. As you develop peace about your own mortality, you will be better equipped to prepare others for their death.

Don't miss the helpful words of I Corinthians 15:35-58.

The world tells us that death is the grim reaper coming to snatch us away. God says to the child of God that our homecoming is precious to him. The door every believer must pass through is the death of this failing body. Passing through this door enables us to put on the new perfect body prepared for us. Even as we pass through this door we are not alone. Jesus is beside us. There is no fear because He comforts us.

As for me, I will behold thy face in righteousness: I shall be satisfied, when I awake, with thy likeness - Psalm 17:15.

Beloved, now are we the sons of God, and it doth not yet appear what we shall be: but we know that, when he shall appear, we shall be like him; for we shall see him as he is - I John 3:2.

Have not I commanded thee? Be strong and of a good courage; be not afraid, neither be thou dismayed: for the Lord thy God is with thee withersoever thou goest - Joshua 1:9.

Precious in the sight of the Lord is the death of his saints - Psalm 116:15.

Yea, though I walk through the valley of the shadow of death, I will fear no evil: for thou art with me; thy rod and thy staff they comfort me - Psalm 23:4.

We are confident, I say, and willing rather to be absent from the body, and to be present with the Lord - II Corinthians 5:8.

For I know that my redeemer liveth, and that he shall stand at the latter day upon the earth: And though after my skin worms destroy this body, yet in my flesh shall I see God - Job 19:25, 26.

For to me to live is Christ, and to die is gain. But if I live in the flesh, this is the fruit of my labour: yet what I shall choose I wot not. For I am in a strait betwixt two, having a desire to depart, and to be with Christ; which is far better -Philippians 1:21-23.

But I would not have you to be ignorant, brethren, concerning them which are asleep, that ye sorrow not, even as others which have no hope. For if we believe that Jesus died and rose again, even so them also which sleep in Jesus will God bring with him, For this we say unto you by the word of the Lord, that we which are alive and remain unto the coming of the Lord shall not prevent them which are asleep. For the Lord himself shall descend from heaven with a shout, with the voice of the archangel, and with the trump of God: and the dead in Christ shall rise first: Then we which are alive and remain shall be caught up together with them in the clouds, to meet the Lord in the air: and so shall we ever be with the Lord. Wherefore comfort one another with these words - 1 Thessalonians 4:13-18.

WHAT ABOUT LONELINESS?

Picture yourself moving into a small room already occupied by a person you've never before met. Professionals walk in and out of your room as they work, and you fight the sensation of being a non-person. You sometimes feel like a street person alone in a big city. This is the reality of professional care living.

Are people in nursing homes lonely? Certainly, but you can help.

Your visits and offers of friendship will help. Go beyond your visit. Read or speak words of comfort from God and your new friends will not be alone when you leave.

> *Nevertheless I tell you the truth; It is expedient for you that I go away; for if I go not away, the Comforter will not come unto you; but if I depart, I will send him unto you - John 16:7.*

> *Grace be unto you, and peace, from God our Father, and from the Lord Jesus Christ. - I Corinthians 1:3.*

> *Thou tellest my wanderings; put thou my tears into thy bottle; are they not in thy book? - Psalm 56:8.*

Reach out first. We all need and want friends. Keep in mind that the only perfect friend is Jesus.

> *A man that hath friends must shew himself friendly; and there is a friend that sticketh closer than a brother - Proverbs 18:24.*

We are to follow Jesus. Many times, He experienced loneliness but He knew the difficulties of the present could produce a harvest of joy in the future.

Behold, the hour cometh, yea, is now come, that ye shall be scattered, every man to his own, and shall leave me alone: and yet I am not alone, because the Father is with me. These things I have spoken unto you, that in me ye might have peace. In the world ye shall have tribulation: but be of good cheer; I have overcome the world - John 16:32, 33.

Wherefore seeing we also are compassed about with so great a cloud of witnesses, let us lay aside every weight, and the sin which doth so easily beset us, and let us run with patience the race that is set before us looking unto Jesus the author and finisher of our faith; who for the joy that was set before him endured the cross, despising the shame, and is set down at the right hand of the throne of God - Hebrews 12:1, 2.

WILL THERE BE JUDGMENT?

Unfortunately, some people think God's only attribute is love. They have never seen or heard scriptures about the wrath of God. This belief lulls people into a false sense of spiritual security. You may encounter people who have postponed making a commitment to God because, as they say, "All roads lead to heaven, just do your best, that's all God wants."

A working knowledge of these verses will be exactly what you need for these situations.

Oh let the wickedness of the wicked come to an end; but establish the just: for the righteous God trieth the hearts and reins - Psalm 7:9.

The wicked shall be turned into hell, and all the nations that forget God - Psalm 9:17.

He, that being often reproved hardeneth his neck, shall suddenly be destroyed, and that without remedy - Proverbs 29:1.

Countless people reject God and His plan of salvation because of their pride. How sad! Life for them has no real meaning, and death is a fearsome specter.

The wicked, through the pride of his countenance, will not seek after God: God is not in all his thoughts - Psalm 10:4.

For what shall it profit a man, if he shall gain the whole world, and lose his own soul? Or what shall a man give in exchange for his soul? - Mark 8:36, 37.

For the wrath of God is revealed from heaven against all ungodliness and unrighteousness of men, who hold the truth in unrighteousness; For the invisible things of him from the creation of the world are clearly seen, being understood by the things that are made, even his eternal power

*and Godhead; so that they are without excuse -
Romans 1:18-20.*

*For we must all appear before the judgment seat
of Christ; that every one may receive the things
done in his body, according to that he hath done,
whether it be good or bad. Knowing therefore
the terror of the Lord, we persuade men; but we
are made manifest unto God; and I trust also are
made manifest in your consciences - II Corinthians 5:10, 11.*

*Be not deceived; God is not mocked: for what-
soever a man soweth, that shall he also reap.
For he that soweth to his flesh shall of the flesh
reap corruption; but he that soweth to the Spirit
shall of the Spirit reap life everlasting -
Galatians 6:7, 8.*

*And as it is appointed unto men once to die, but
after this the judgment - Hebrews 9:27.*

*Knowing this first, that there shall come in the
last days scoffers, walking after their own lusts,
And saying, Where is the promise of his coming?
for since the fathers fell asleep, all things continue as they were from the beginning of the creation. For this they willingly are ignorant of, that
by the word of God the heavens were of old, and
the earth standing out of the water and in the
water: Whereby the world that then was, being
overflowed with water, perished: But the*

heavens and the earth, which are now, by the same word are kept in store, reserved unto fire against the day of judgment and perdition of ungodly men. Seeing then that all these things shall be dissolved, what manner of persons ought ye to be in all holy conversation and godliness - II Peter 3:3-11.

And I saw a great white throne, and him that sat on it, from whose face the earth and the heaven fled away; and there was found no place for them. And I saw the dead, small and great, stand before God; and the books were opened: and another book was opened, which is the book of life; and the dead were judged out of those things which were written in the books, according to their works. And the sea gave up the dead which were in it; and death and hell delivered up the dead which were in them: and they were judged every man according to their works. And death and hell were cast into the lake of fire. This is the second death. And whosoever was not found written in the book of life was cast into the lake of fire - Revelation 20:11-15.

A life lived rejecting God's revealed will says, "I hate God."

He that walketh in his uprightness feareth the Lord: but he that is perverse in his ways despiseth him - Proverbs 14:2.

WISDOM - GOD'S WAY

As a volunteer in nursing homes, you'll need wisdom and lots of it! After reading these scriptures, you'll see God is not short on wisdom and He loves to share it. The whole book of Proverbs is full of inspirational verses on wisdom. Read especially Proverbs 2:1-11.

Trust in the Lord with all thine heart; and lean not unto thine own understanding. In all thy ways acknowledge him, and he shall direct thy paths - Proverbs 3:5, 6.

If any of you lack wisdom, let him ask of God, that giveth to all men liberally, and upbraideth not; and it shall be given him. But let him ask in faith, nothing wavering. For he that wavereth is like a wave of the sea driven with the wind and tossed. For let not that man think that he shall receive anything of the Lord. A double minded man is unstable in all his ways - James 1:5-8.

Behold, I have taught you statutes and judgments, even as the Lord my God commanded me, that ye should do so in the land whither ye go to possess it. Keep therefore and do them; for this is your wisdom and your understanding in the sight of the nations, which shall hear all these statutes and say, Surely this great nation is a wise and understanding people - Deuteronomy 4:5, 6.

The mouth of the righteous speaketh wisdom, and his tongue talketh of judgment - Psalm 37:30.

Behold, thou desirest truth in the inward parts: and in the hidden part thou shalt make me to know wisdom - Psalm 51:6.

And I, brethren, when I came to you, came not with excellency of speech or of wisdom, declaring unto you the testimony of God. For I determined not to know anything among you, save Jesus Christ, and him crucified. And I was with you in weakness, and in fear, and in much trembling. And my speech and my preaching was not with enticing words of man's wisdom, but in demonstration of the Spirit and of power: That your faith should not stand in the wisdom of men, but in the power of God. Howbeit we speak wisdom among them that are perfect: yet not the wisdom of this world, nor of the princes of this world, that come to nought: But we speak the wisdom of God in a mystery, even the hidden wisdom, which God ordained before the world unto our glory: Which none of the princes of this world knew: for had they known it, they would not have crucified the Lord of glory - I Corinthians 2:1-8.

WITNESSING

Preparedness is the key here. God is so good. He doesn't tell us to memorize the whole Bible before we can represent Him. Be wise, though. John 3:16 is not the only scripture you will ever need.

God suggests in II Timothy 2:16 that if we want to avoid shame as we work for Him, we must expect to study His Word. A construction worker who is only skilled in hammering is not very useful. He could nail but never measure a doorway, cut a piece of wood, or turn a screw. So, we as Christians are expected to increase our skills in God's Word in order to expand our usefulness to him.

These selected verses will encourage and equip you for the "job" of witnessing. God offers wisdom and boldness to speak. You will see results. Learn to delight in God's Word. Make it an integral part of your life and He will lead you to success.

It's a wonderful privilege to pray with people as they ask God to receive them as His child.

Blessed is the man that walketh not in the counsel of the ungodly, nor standeth in the way of the sinners, not sitteth in the seat of the scornful. But his delight is the law of the Lord; and in his law doth he meditate day and night. And he shall be like a tree planted by the rivers of water, that bringeth forth his fruit in his season; his leaf also shall not wither; and whatsoever he doeth shall prosper - Psalm 1:1-3.

But sanctify the Lord God in your hearts: and be ready always to give an answer to every man that asketh you a reason of the hope that is in you with meekness and fear - I Peter 3:15.

And my tongue shall speak of thy righteousness, and of thy praise all the day long - Psalm 35:28.

I will go in the strength of the Lord God: I will make mention of thy righteuosness , even of thine only - Psalm 71:16.

Make me to understand the way of thy precepts: so shall I talk of thy wondrous works - Psalm 119:27.

The Lord God hath given me the tongue of the learned, that I should know how to speak a word in season to him that is weary: he waketh morning by morning, he waketh mine ear to hear as the learned - Isaiah 50:4.

A word fitly spoken is like apples of gold in pictures of silver - Proverbs 25:11.

For our rejoicing is this, the testimony of our conscience, that in simplicity and godly sincerity, not with fleshly wisdom, but by the grace of God, we have had our conversation in the world, and more abundantly to you-ward - II Corinthians 1:12.

How beautiful upon the mountains are the feet of him that bringeth good tidings, that publisheth peace; that bringeth good tidings of good, that publisheth salvation; that saith unto Zion, Thy God reigneth! - Isaiah 52:7.

They that sow in tears shall reap in joy. He that goeth forth and weepeth, bearing precious seed, shall doubtless come again with rejoicing, bringing his sheaves with him - Psalm 126:5, 6.

And let us not be weary in well doing: for in due season we shall reap, if we faint not - Galatians 6:9.

I will instruct thee and teach thee in the way which thou shalt go: I will guide thee with mine eye - Psalm 32:8.

The Lord is my light and my salvation; whom shall I fear? The Lord is the strength of my life; of whom shall I be afraid? - Psalm 27:1.

For I am not ashamed of the gospel of Christ: for it is the power of God unto salvation to every one that believeth; to the Jew first, and also to the Greek - Romans 1:16.

Remember this as you look for opportunities to minister spiritually to people: no matter what facade people wear, only a relationship with God through Jesus Christ produces peace. God says so.

There is peace, saith the Lord, unto the wicked - Isaiah 48:22.

As a witness, are you good salt? When you realize that salt is a preservative, a healing agent, adds flavor and causes thirst, then you like the nickname, "salt".

*Ye are the salt of the earth: but if the salt have
lost his savour, but to be cast out, and to be trod-
den under foot of men - Matthew 5:13.*

We are to shine by reflecting the light of the world,
Jesus. This brings glory to God Who is light.

*Ye are the light of the world. A city that is set on
an hill cannot be hid. Neither do men light a
candle, and put it under a bushel, but not on a
candlestick; and it giveth light unto all that are
in the house. Let your light so shine before men,
that they may see your good works, and glorify
your Father which is in heaven - Matthew 5:14-
16.*

As we live out the words in the following verses our
witness becomes effective.

*Let love be without dissimulation. Abhor that
which is evil; cleave to that which is good. Be
kindly affectioned one to another with brotherly
love; in honour preferring one another; not
slothful in business; fervent in spirit; serving the
Lord; Rejoicing in hope; patient in tribulation;
continuing instant in prayer; distributing to the
necessity of saints; given to hospitality. Bless
them which persecute you: bless, and curse not.
Rejoice with them that do rejoice, and weep with
them that weep. Be of the same mind one toward*

another. Mind not high things, but condescend to men of low estate. Be not wise in your own conceits - Romans 12:9-16.

There is no use to explain Bible doctrine to someone who has not yet placed their faith in Jesus. God says they can't understand. Rather, through the leading of the Holy Spirit, explain salvation to them.

But the natural man receiveth not the things of the spirit of God; for they are foolishness unto him: neither can he know them, because they are spiritually discerned - I Corinthians 2:14.

WORD OF GOD

This topic is important for volunteers! As Christians, we go through life representing God, the Creator of the universe. What an unbelievable honor! What an awesome responsibility! There is only one possible way to correctly represent anyone in conversation. We must know the individual and what their views are regarding every subject discussed.

The Bible teaches us God's viewpoint. His Spirit helps us to recall the right words at the right time. The only weakness in this plan is that we cannot recall words we've never read. His Word is authority and power. For inspiration as you prepare to represent Him, read the following verses.

This book of law shall not depart my mouth; but thou shalt meditate therein day and night, that thou mayest observe to do according to all that is written therein: for then thou shalt make thy way prosperous, and then thou shalt have good success - Joshua 1:8.

Who so despiseth the word shall be destroyed: but he that feareth the commandment shall be rewarded - Proverbs 13:13.

Whom shall he teach knowledge? and whom shall he make to understand doctrine? them that are weaned from the milk, and drawn from the breasts. For precept must be upon precept, precept upon precept; line upon line, line upon line; here a little, and there a little - Isaiah 28:9, 10.

Study to shew thyself approved unto God, a workman that needeth not to be ashamed, rightly dividing the Word of truth - II Timothy 2:15.

As newborn babes, desire the sincere milk of the word, that ye may grow thereby - I Peter 2:2.

Be careful not to elevate religious writings and history to the same level of God's Word, the Bible.

Howbeit in vain do they worship me, teaching for doctrines the commandments of men - Mark 7:7.

Wherefore the Lord said, Forasmuch as this people draw near me with their mouth, and with their lips do honour me, but have removed their heart far from me, and their fear toward me is taught by the precept of men - Isaiah 29:13.

And that from a child thou hast known the holy scriptures which are able to make thee wise unto salvation through faith which is in Christ Jesus. All scripture is given by inspiration of God, and is profitable for doctrine, for reproof, for correction, for instruction in righteousness: That the man of God may be perfect, thoroughly furnished unto all good works - II Timothy 3:15-17.

Knowing this first, that no prophecy of the scripture is of any private interpretation. For the prophecy came not in old time by the will of man: but holy men of God spake as they were moved by the Holy Ghost - Peter 1:20, 21.

Use the Words of God as you speak. They have power.

Is not my word like as a fire? saith the Lord; and like a hammer that breaketh the rock in pieces? - Jeremiah 23:29.

For the word of God is quick, and powerful, and sharper than any twoedged sword, piercing even to the dividing asunder of soul and spirit, and of the joints and marrow, and is a discerner of the thoughts and intents of the heart - Hebrews 4:12.

Chapter 13

DO I DARE?
(Questions For Review)

Review of Chapter 1 - Is There A Need?

1. What was Ruth's question?_____

_____

_____

2. What might you reply to her? _____

_____

_____

3. Do you feel Christians have an invitation or an obligation to visit the elderly?_____

_____

_____

Explain why you think this is so:_____

_____

_____

4. How did you feel when Ruth expressed her dismay?

_____

_____

5. Choose a favorite verse in Chapter 12 that relates to
   the need for volunteers from each of these three
   topics.

   Temporary Bodies:_____

   _____

   Life is Short:_____

   _____

   Self-Worth:_____

   _____

Review of Chapter 2 - Who is Qualified to Go?

1. What are management's feelings about volunteers?

   _____

2. Can you list any of the reasons Christians have not
   been   more involved in rest home ministries?_____

   _____

3. What personality is best suited for visiting? _____

   _____

4. How much "pressure" is there to perform perfectly when ministering to the elderly?_____

_____

5. List the verse from "Loneliness" that you would like to share with a nursing home resident: _____

_____

6. Which scripture from "Love is a Command" speaks to you   most about the love you should have toward the elderly?

_____

7. From the "Word of God" list, write the verse that God impressed on your heart._____

_____

Review of Chapter 3 -
Where Are These Places and Why Do They Exist?

1. List the three main types of homes for the elderly.

_____

_____

2. What kinds of people would you expect to meet in each   type?_____

_____

_____

_____

3. Approximately how many nursing and convalescent homes are there in comfortable traveling distance from you?_____

4. Do you ordinarily drive past any of these homes? _____

5. As you go by, have you ever noticed any of the residents?_____

_____

Were they alone?_____

What were they doing?_____

_____

6. Have you ever been touched by any perceived loneliness in what you saw?_____

7. Why do you think you felt as you did?_____

_____

_____

_____

8. What changes in our society have affected the use of long term care facilities? _____

_____

_____

_____

9. How and why has our generation changed its evaluation of older people?_____

_____

_____

10. How do these perceptions affect the seniors?_____

_____

_____

11. From the scriptures listed under "What about Death" are there any that you could share with an oldster?

_____

_____

_____

12. How do you feel about "Suffering?"_____

_____

_____

_____

What scriptures help? _____

_____

Review of Chapter 4 - What Goes on Inside?

1. Describe the interiors of nursing homes you have seen or read about._____

_____

_____

2. Give added insight from this chapter about the management. _____

_____

_____

3. Picture yourself residing permanently in one of the rooms. How do you feel?_____

_____

_____

4. What do you like about being there?_____

_____

_____

_____

5. Is there anything that disturbed you? _____

_____

_____

Could it be helped by a visiting Christian? _____

_____

6. "Long Life" is a fitting topic to study. Does any verse stand out to you? _____

_____

_____

_____

7. So many wonderful verses about "Salvation"! List the   the ones most meaningful to you and also those you might like to share:_____

_____

_____

_____

_____

Review of Chapter 5 - Why Me?

1. What would you list as the three most important reasons for visiting? _____

   _____

   _____

   _____

2. How do you feel about what you have just listed? ___

   _____

3. Do you believe that God could use you to fulfill even one on your list?_____

   Could you eventually fulfill all three with God's assistance?_____

   _____

4. What do you think are the major reasons Christians have not responded to the needs of people in long-term care   homes?_____

   _____

   Can you think of additional reasons?_____

   _____

   _____

5. How could the title of "missionary" be used to describe a resident's activities?_____

   _____

   _____

6. Could this title also be suitable for a nursing home volunteer? _____

   Why?_____

   _____

   _____

7. Which verse on "Faith" prompts you to respond to the needs of the elderly? _____

   _____

8. Write out two verses that come from the lists of "Judgment" and "Religion" whose principles could be used in when dealing with the elderly:_____

   _____

Review of Chapter 6 - Using your gifts

1. What are the seven gifts of the spirit as listed in Romans 12?_____

   _____

2. Out of this list which describes you?_____

   _____

3. What ideas on visiting seem most suitable for your gift application? _____

4. How many types of weekly programs can you record?

   _____

   _____

5. Name as many ideas for impromptu visits as you can:

_____

_____

6. Did you find an important principle to help in witnessing? Describe this principle: _____

_____

_____

7. What story or episode in Chapter 6 would you like to have been in yourself?_____

Why?_____

_____

8. Would you only feel comfortable encouraging others to visit by exhorting and organizing them or could you actually go yourself?_____

_____

9. How do you think you could interest others? _____

_____

10. Why should children be involved in this ministry?

_____

_____

11. What practical ways can this be accomplished?

_____

_____

12. Write out one verse from each of the four categories that either prompts you to action or gives you something to share with the elderly.

Fear/Peace: _____

_____

Forgiveness - What a Relief!: _____

_____

Praise God!:_____

_____

Witnessing: _____

_____

Review of Chapter 7 - Getting Started

1. Try to list the seven things to do to get started:_____

_____

_____

2. Record the ones you could not accomplish: _____

_____

_____

3. Write down two "Promises" either from those listed or select one of your own from the Bible. Choose one for the elderly, and one for yourself:_____

_____

_____

Review of Chapter 8 - Room Etiquette

1. How many helpful hints for visiting can you remember?   Make a list of them. There are more than 40!

_____

_____

_____

_____

_____

_____

_____

2. What wonderful biblical subjects to read about!   List your favorite verse(s) on:

Heaven: _____

Prayer: _____

Rewards: _____

Review of Chapter 9 - Lots Of Stories

1. In the chapter of stories, what episode evoked the strongest feeling in you? _____

_____

Tell why: _____

_____

_____

_____

2. What ways other than those listed in the book could be used to minister?_____

_____

_____

3. All people need Assurance and Wisdom. List a verse from each topic that you feel God wants you to absorb:_____

_____

_____

Review of Chapter 10 - More Stories - Surprising Adventures

1. Were you surprised at some of the encounters in this chapter? _____

Which ones? _____
Why? _____

_____

_____

2. If any of the people you visit behaved as these people did, could you handle them?_____

Could God? _____
How could you prepare for these difficult visits?

_____

_____

_____

3. Which scriptures and comments, do you think will be the most helpful to the people you will visit? _____

_____

_____

_____

_____

_____

_____

4. Tell how you might like to use them: _____

_____

_____

5. Which verses encouraged you the most to go and visit?

_____

_____

_____

6. Will you be able to memorize any?_____

7. Which verse do you think will help you as a volunteer?_____

_____

_____

_____

8. Why?_____

_____

_____

_____

9. In summary, these are my personal feelings about ministering to the elderly:_____

_____

_____

_____

_____

_____

_____

_____

_____

_____

_____

_____

_____

_____

_____

RESOURCES

1. William E. Hulme, Vintage Years (Philadelphia, Pennsylvania: The Westminster Press, 1986).

2. Paul B. Maves, Faith for the Older Years (Minneapolis, Minnesota: Augsburg Publishing House, 1986).

3. John Gillies, Care Giving (Wheaton, Illinois: Harold Shaw Publishers, 1988).

4. Tom and Penny McCormick, Nursing Home Ministry (Grand Rapids, Michigan: Zondervan Publishing House, 1982).

5. Fish, Sharon and Judith Allen Shelly, Spiritual Care: The Nurse's Role (Downers Grove, Illinois: Inter-Varsity Press, 1978).

6. Keys, Joel T, Our Older Friends (Philadelphia, Pennsylvania: Fortress Press, 1983).

7. Sollenberger, Opal Hutchins, I Chose to Live in a Nursing Home (Elgin, Illinois: David C. Cook Publishing, 1980).

8. Rodgers, "Corky" H.B. Project Compassion For The Elderly (Denver, Colorado: Good News Communications, 1984).

9. Gilhuis, Cornelis, Conversations On Growing Older (Grand Rapids, Michigan: William B. Eerdmans Publishing Co., 1977).

10. Syverson, Betty Groth, "Bible Readings for Caregivers", (Augsburg Publishing House, Minneapolis, Minnesota, 1987

11. Haakenson, Herm, "The Sonshine Society", P. O. Box 327, Lynnwood, Washington 98036, 1976 (excellent resource for convalescent ministry).

12. Kinman, Chaplain Dwight L., "Love Thy Neighbor Ministries", P.O. Box 386, Canby, Oregon 97013

ENDNOTES

1. John 17:4

2. Matthew 25:36, 40.

3. I Thessalonians 5:14.

4. Romans 5:6.

5. Romans 15:2

6. James 2:14-18

7. "Who Can Afford a Nursing Home?", <u>Consumer Reports</u>, May 1988, pp. 300-309.

8. <u>Statistical Abstract of the U.S.</u>, (1989 U.S. Dept. of Commerce) pp 766, chart 1348.

9. <u>The Subtle Revolution</u>, Ralph E. Smith, ed. (Washington, D.C.: The Urban Institute, 1979), 3.

10. <u>Statistical Abstract of the U.S.</u> (1989 U.S. Dept. of Commerce.) pp. 385, chart 637.

11. Pat Moore with Charles Paul Conn, <u>Disguised</u> (Waco, TX: Word Book, 1985).

12. Deuteronomy 26:12, 13.

13. Proverbs 4:18.

14. Philippians 4:11.

15. Psalm 92:14.

16. Ephesians 5:16.

17. Romans 1:18-20.

18. Matthew 6:19-21.

19. Colossians 3:2.

20. James 1:27.

21. Tom and Penny McCormick, <u>Nursing Home Ministry</u> (Grand Rapids, MI: Zondervan Publishing House, 1982).

22. Colossians 3:23.

23. Deuteronomy 6:6-8.

24. Proverbs 6:21-22.

25. <u>Mother Goose Gospel, Inc</u>. (Brentwood Music, Brentwood, TN, 1988).

26. <u>Hymns for Kids</u> (The Benson Company, Inc., Nashville, TN, 1988).

27. Psalm 119:50.

28. <u>Love thy Neighbor Ministries,</u> P.O. Box 386, Canby, OR 97013.

29. Ephesians 5:16.

30. James 2:19.

31. James 1:5.

32. Joshua 1:9.

33. Deuteronomy 31:6.

34. I Thessalonians 5:22.

35. Psalm 37:4.

36. Proverbs 17:22.

37. II Corinthians 4:16 .

38. I John 4:12.

39. Matthew 17:20b.

40. II Corinthians 9:6-8 .

41. Psalm 23:4.

42. I Peter 5:8.

43. I John 4:4.

44. John 3:16.

45. Psalm 100:1.

46. James 5:16.

47. Psalm 66:18.

48. Proverbs 28:9.

49. I John 1:9.

• NEW RELEASE •
NOW AVAILABLE ON VIDEO

"A Song for Grandmother"

Julie Grimstad, Director of the Center for the Rights of the Terminally Ill, reviewed this video:

"Well done! Inspiring! Enchanting! Exactly what we've been waiting for! Every group which ministers to the elderly, every pastor, every Sunday school teacher, and every deacon must see this film and share it with others. Then, I believe, Christians will reach out to our elderly brothers and sisters, to touch them with love and dignity."

In a review, Carol Goodheart said,

"A Song for Grandmother" offers a very tangible, simple and exciting solution. "A Song for Grand-mother" will bring tears to your eyes, but joy to your heart. See it! Tell your friends to see it! This is an important film."

In addition to the book and the video, Jeremiah Films is offering a mobilization manual called, "Compassion in Action." This manual is designed to assist ministry groups in their application of **"A Song for Grandmother"** video and book.

CONTACT YOUR LOCAL
CHRISTIAN BOOKSTORE OR CALL:
(800)828-2290
In California **(800)633-0869**

For a free catalog call the above number or write:
Jeremiah Films
P. O. Box 1712, Hemet, CA 92343